JURGEN WOLFF

Your Writing Coach

From Concept to Character, From Pitch to Publication

Everything you need to know about writing novels, non-fiction, new media, scripts and short stories

NICHOLAS BREALEY
PUBLISHING
LONDON · BOSTON

Contents

Praise for

Your Writing Coach

"With compassion, wit and the wisdom gleaned from a long and successful writing career, Jurgen Wolff guides you, step by step, on the inner and outer journey to writing success. An invaluable tool for the aspiring writer."
Robert Cochran, co-creator and executive producer, 24

"*Your Writing Coach* pays as much attention to writers as to what they write and should help seasoned pros as much as it will help beginners. Jurgen Wolff is wise and constructive when it comes to such issues as fear of failure, your inner critic, and rejection, as well as brainstorming and finding the conditions in which to work. Highly recommended."
Julian Friedmann, writer's agent, Blake Friedmann, and editor, ScriptWriter *magazine*

"This book is the real deal—no fluff or padding, just concentrated insider knowledge. By far the best book on writing I have read."
Rupert Widdicombe, writer and journalist

"This book is an antidote to the bad advice aspiring writers are often given. There are only two books on writing I recommend— Stephen King's and this one."
William F. Owen, author of Blackfoot Is Missing

"This book will help you find the insights of the writing craft. Pick it up and let it guide you to success."
Xavier Koller, Academy Award-winning director, Journey of Hope

"Jurgen Wolff demystifies the writing process in a series of easy-to-understand steps guaranteed to make you a better writer."
Phil Doran, author of the bestselling The Reluctant Tuscan

Dedicated to you
and your success as a writer

First published by
Nicholas Brealey Publishing in 2007

3–5 Spafield Street	20 Park Plaza, Suite 1115A
Clerkenwell, London	Boston
EC1R 4QB, UK	MA 02116, USA
Tel: +44 (0)20 7239 0360	Tel: (888) BREALEY
Fax: +44 (0)20 7239 0370	*Fax: (617) 523 3708*

www.nicholasbrealey.com
www.timetowrite.com

© Jurgen Wolff 2007
The right of Jurgen Wolff to be identified as the author of this work
has been asserted in accordance with the Copyright, Designs and
Patents Act 1988.

ISBN-13: 978-1-85788-367-1
ISBN-10: 1-85788-367-5

British Library Cataloguing in Publication Data
A catalogue record for this book is available from the
British Library.

Library of Congress Cataloging-in-Publication Data

Wolff, Jurgen, 1956-
  Your writing coach : from concept to character, from pitch to
publication; everything you need to know about writing novels, non-
fiction, new media, scripts, and short stories / Jurgen Wolff.
    p. cm.
  ISBN-13: 978-1-85788-367-1
  ISBN-10: 1-85788-367-5
  1. Authorship. 2. Authorship--Marketing. I. Title.

PN147.W56 2007
808'.02--dc22

2006038867

Printed in the UK by Clays Ltd, St Ives plc.

Introduction

"When love and skill work together, expect a masterpiece."
—*John Ruskin*

Do you want to start writing or to write more, and more skill-fully? You've come to the right place, because I'd like to be your writing coach and guide you through the entire process, including a lot of aspects that other writing books never tell you about.

If something's been stopping you from writing, it's probably down to one of the fears I reveal in Chapter 1, where you can also discover how to overcome every one of them. Then I'll help you decide what you are best suited to write, whether it's short stories, articles, novels, non-fiction books, or scripts. You'll also find out how to take advantage of your knowledge and life experience in your writing.

Then we turn to the actual process of writing, starting with unique right-brain creativity techniques that you can use to generate an endless flow of ideas. Then you'll learn how the "magic why" can produce a blueprint of your story, and how to create wonderful, vivid characters. I'll share with you the Q/A technique, a tool you can use to hook your readers and keep them engaged all the way through your book, story, or script. You'll learn story secrets that help you structure your material, and techniques to make your language vivid and compelling. And you'll see how you can evaluate your first draft and rewrite effectively and efficiently.

The third part of the book covers a number of crucial topics that are often ignored. These include how to get your friends and family to understand and support your creative activities, how to create a great writing space for yourself, how to use your writing time most effectively, and how to motivate yourself when your energy starts to flag. Every writer faces rejection from time to time, so I'll show you how to deal with critics, including the one who is usually the harshest of all—your inner critic. With the neuro-linguistic programming technique in Chapter 12, you'll be able to transform the inner critic into a constructive inner guide—the key to avoiding or overcoming writer's block.

In the final section of the book you'll learn the secrets of marketing yourself and your work, beyond the normal methods that most other writers are using. There's also a chapter on new media, which offer tremendous opportunities for writers smart enough to find out about them. And we finish with a chapter on how to create and enjoy the writing life.

One of the best features of this book isn't in the book itself. Every chapter has a bonus that you'll be able to access on the website www.yourwritingcoach.com by typing in the code word at the end of that chapter. These bonuses include a video interview with Robert Cochran, the co-creator of the international hit series *24*, telling you about writing thrilling scripts; another with agent Julian Friedmann candidly discussing what agents look for in clients; and another with a mystery writer from Murder Squad, a group of UK crime writers who have figured out how to get free publicity for themselves and their books. There are additional audio interviews, demonstrations of writing and rewriting techniques, and much more—all at no extra charge to buyers of this book.

Once you've read the book, if you still have questions you are welcome to email me at jurgenwolff@gmail.com and I'll do my best to answer them, because I'm serious about being your writing coach. I know from my own 25 years' experience of writing articles, books (*Do Something Different*, among others), scripts for television (including *Benson*, *Family Ties*, and *Relic Hunter*), and films (*The Real Howard Spitz*, starring Kelsey Grammer and Amanda Donohoe) that writing can be the most satisfying creative activity in the world—and it pays pretty well, too! I'd like to share with you all the lessons I've learned (some of them the hard way) and help you on the road to your writing success. Are you ready to start?

PART I
READY, STEADY...

"All glory comes from daring to begin."

—*Eugene F. Ware*

If something has been holding you back from writing, it's probably a fear of some kind. In this part, we take the bull by the horns by confronting and banishing the fears that typically keep talented people from expressing themselves as writers. Then we find out what specific type of writing suits you best. Finally, we explore how who you are and what you know can guide you in selecting what stories to tell.

1

No More Fear, No More Excuses

"To do anything in this world worth doing, we must not stand back shivering and thinking of the cold and danger, but jump in, and scramble through as best we can."
—*Sidney Smith*

A good coach should prepare you for the obstacles that may lie ahead, and I know the number one obstacle you will face on your road to success. It's *you*.

Years ago there was a wonderful comic strip called "Pogo," and one famous line from it was, "We have met the enemy, and he is us." It's true. Yes, it can be hard to think of the right word, find the right agent, and put up with dumb decisions from editors or studio executives, but the main problems we face are generated by ourselves. Most of the time, these stem from our fears.

You may feel certain this does not apply to you, but in many cases the fear is hidden not only from others, but also from ourselves as would-be writers. Therefore, I respectfully suggest that you don't skip this chapter. If any of the fears mentioned here ring true, they may be at the root of your inability so far to write as much or as well as you'd like. Fortunately, as you'll see, there is a way to overcome each of these fears. The best strategy is to face them right now, head on, before we get on the nuts and bolts of writing and selling your work. Here they are, the Big Seven Fears and the ways to conquer them.

The fear of rejection

This is by far the most common fear of writers and artists of all kinds—in fact, of all human beings. Generally, when you stop yourself from doing anything, at the heart of that self-sabotage is the fear that you (or what you create) will be rejected.

When you were young, maybe your mother or father encouraged you to take a chance on doing something by saying, "The worst that can happen is that they say no." What they didn't realize was that this *is* the worst that can happen. If you have a memory of asking someone out when you were a teenager, and that person said no, you'll probably still be able to call up that feeling of teeth-grinding, I-wish-I-could-just-sink-into-the-earth humiliation. Unfortunately, children quickly become expert at ridiculing others who are different—too fat, too thin, too tall, too short, too geeky, too anything. You learn to fit in, to do what everybody else is doing, desperate not to stand out. Of course, the irony is that every breakthrough, in writing or in any other field, comes from doing something different from what the average person is doing.

Here's the hard truth about rejection: You can't avoid it. There isn't a single successful writer who hasn't had work rejected at one point or another. Most of them had many, many rejections before they had their first success. Here are a few examples:

- It took J.K. Rowling a year to find a publisher for the first Harry Potter book. There was only one offer, from Bloomsbury, for £2,500 (about $4,900). At the end of their meeting her publisher's parting words were, "You'll never make any money out of children's books, Jo."
- Melody Beattie's non-fiction book *Co-Dependent No More* was turned down by 20 publishers. It went on to sell five million copies.
- Joanne Harris wrote three books that failed to find a publisher. Her fourth book, the novel *Chocolat*, became an

international bestseller and spawned an equally successful film.

⌀ John Grisham's first novel, *A Time to Kill*, was rejected by 15 agents and 26 publishers before Wynwood Press agreed to publish it—in an edition of 5,000 copies. The book didn't become a bestseller until Grisham's next three were hugely successful.

⌀ Wilbur Smith's first novel found no publisher, and he decided that writing wasn't for him. Eighteen months later, his agent convinced him to have another try. That book sold, and since then his novels have sold 84 million copies.

I could fill this entire book with similar stories. Rejection comes with the territory. If you expect rejection and remember not to take it personally, it loses some of its sting. Remind yourself that the people who are judging you are fallible (let's spend a happy moment imagining how the publishers who turned down J.K. Rowling must be feeling just about now...).

That's not to say it won't hurt when the big fat envelope containing your manuscript comes back again, or when agents say they don't even want to read your material. It will, but you'll get over it. Here's what Norman Mailer has to say about this, in his book *The Spooky Art*:

> "More sensitive than others in the beginning, we have to develop the will, the stamina, the determination, and the insensitivity to take critical abuse. A good writer, therefore, does well to see himself as a strong weak person, full of brave timidity, sensitive and insensitive. In effect, we have to learn to live in the world with its bumps and falls and occasionally startling rewards while protecting the core of what once seemed a frighteningly perishable sensitivity."

In other words, you can't just try to transform yourself into someone with such a hard shell that you no longer feel any pain. If you do, you lose the very part of yourself that allows you to create insightful, emotional, touching stories and books and scripts. The two parts of yourself have to co-exist. Fortunately, there are some excellent techniques for doing this. One is always to be working on the next thing. When you finish one writing project and start to send it out, get right to work on the next one. Your creative juices will be flowing and when the first one is rejected, it's much easier to think, "Well, that one may or may not be published eventually, but the one I'm working on now is sure to be a masterpiece." Emotionally, there is nothing worse than feeling your entire career is riding on one project and waiting day after day to hear whether the people to whom you've submitted it actually want it.

The fear that it won't be good enough

This fear sometimes stops people before they even start. Such people measure their ideas against the best writing of all time. Can what you intend to write possibly attain the stature of the works of Shakespeare, Conrad, or Hemingway? Probably not (although you never know). So what's the point of writing it in the first place? If you use this line of reasoning, it's almost certain you'll never get started.

If your pattern is to compare yourself to the greatest authors of all time, there are two ways to get over it. One is to remember that you never know what will stand the test of time. Shakespeare was writing popular entertainment, and probably would be astonished to find his plays still being read and performed 400 years later. If you're worried about how posterity will judge your work, accept that you can't possibly know this anyway.

On a more down-to-earth level, it's helpful to remind yourself that your writing doesn't have to be great literature to have value to your readers. It's unlikely that the books of John Grisham or Danielle Steele will ever feature in many literature courses, yet they have given pleasure to millions. Even the Harry Potter books are looked down on by a number of literary critics, yet all around the world they have rekindled children's interest in reading. If you're writing non-fiction, surely you can think of dozens of examples of books, like *How to Win Friends and Influence People*, that are short on literary merit, but that have helped or inspired millions of people. Richard Carlson, whose series of *Don't Sweat the Small Stuff* books has sold millions, told interviewer Judith Spelman:

> "I don't pretend to be really intellectual. I don't offer psycho-babble. I just write about the very practical and ordinary things and that's why people relate to it."

If your pattern is stopping partway through your project, perhaps you are measuring what you've written against the pristine, perfect vision of it that you had at the start. For example, maybe you wanted to write a book that would illuminate the thoughts and feelings of a woman who is abandoned by her husband and left to raise their handicapped child alone. Halfway through, you read what you've written so far and realize that the characters aren't as alive as you'd hoped they would be, or the plot has some holes in it, or your prose isn't as vibrant as you imagined. At this point, it's easy to give up—why carry on when clearly you're not fulfilling your own vision? Sometimes at this stage a new idea occurs to you, a new story that is, as yet, perfect. So you put aside the half-finished draft and start writing the new story... until, halfway through that one, the same thing happens. After a few instances of this, it's easy to come to the conclusion that you're wasting your time with this writing business and give up.

If you stop yourself by comparing your partly finished book to the ideal you had in mind when you started, consider this: Would you feel disappointed by a 10-year-old boy because he's not going out every day earning a living? Presumably you'd say of course not, he's just a child, he's not an adult yet, why would I expect him to have a career and earn his own way? Your partly finished book is also a child. It becomes a grown-up when it's completed and has been rewritten and polished. That's the time to assess it, not now.

It's also important to remember that it's extremely rare for any artist or writer or architect or other creative person to feel that their final product matches up to their original dream. I'm sure Michelangelo looked up at the ceiling of the Sistine Chapel and thought it could have been just that little bit better. If you accept this as an inevitable part of the creative process, you stop punishing yourself for your supposed failings. The positive aspect of this phenomenon is that it can spur you to move on to your next project, hoping and planning to get closer to realizing your dream next time. You may never arrive, but that desire keeps you travelling hopefully, and the by-product of that journey can be books that entertain or inspire or instruct a dozen people or a million.

For some writers thinking through the logic of this process is enough; others find that they have a strong inner critic who resists mere logic. If you're one of those people, you'll find the solution in Chapter 12, "Tame the Wild Inner (and Outer) Critic."

The fear of success

Everybody understands why someone might be afraid to fail; it's a bit more difficult to understand why some people are afraid of success. The reason is that we tend to fear change, and success is one type of change. Maybe we're afraid that our old friends won't like us any more, or that we won't be able to cope with the demands of fame and fortune. Or maybe we worry that in the public spotlight our failings will be exposed.

The fact is that the only constant is change. Whether or not you succeed as a writer, you will lose some friends and gain others, you will have money pressures (having too little or too much for comfort), and at times you will feel vulnerable.

As far as fortune is concerned, if you earn a lot you always have the option of giving it away. If you don't like being rich, you can choose to go back to being poorer. However, the odds are you won't mind it. As someone has pointed out, "Money can't buy happiness, but it can make unhappiness much more comfortable."

With fame, writers have a big advantage over actors. A very successful actor is recognized by millions of people. The writer who is read by millions still can choose to keep a low public profile. Most readers don't even know what their favorite authors look like, other than the picture on the back cover. Being a bestselling author may open the door to fame, but you don't have to go through it.

The fear of revealing too much

Writers sometimes panic when they realize that the book or script they are writing is a lot more personal than they intended. It may not be strictly autobiographical in terms of dates, times, and names, but their innermost fears, shames, and longings are making their way into the work.

In one way, of course, this is great news. When such deep feelings are reflected in a work it's much more likely to strike a responsive chord in readers. The books you love probably are the ones that made you think the author understood you, that he or she is a kindred spirit. If you don't open yourself up in this way, it's unlikely your words will have much emotional weight. Many writers have said that writing is a kind of therapy. Putting their fears and passions into a book and perhaps coming up with a story that reflects how things should have worked out, rather than how they actually did, can be a healing process. Science fiction and fantasy pioneer Ray Bradbury delivered an invocation at a Humanitas Prize gathering, saying:

> *"Help us to know that only in our loves can we create and out of that creation change some stray, small part of the world we touch."*

Readers don't have some kind of X-ray vision that tells them which part of what you've written is true and which part you've made up. Furthermore, mostly they won't care. It's not the author's experience they're thinking about and sharing, it's the character's.

A separate but related issue is whether family and friends will recognize you or themselves in your work. People know themselves so little that some will see themselves in characters you based on someone totally different, and others will fail to recognize themselves in characters you did base on them. Naturally, you have to avoid a portrayal that is libellous, but beyond that you can't really worry about it. Allow the story to guide you, give your work the feelings it requires, and let the characters come alive. And when it's all done, if someone asks where you got the idea for a particular character, you always have the option of lying. I'm not saying I ever do this, but when my play *Killing Mother* was produced, I did tell my mother that it was based on the story a friend told me about his mother...

The fear that you have only one book in you

Most people have heard of publishing's sophomore curse: Often a second novel is less successful than the first. Frequently, this happens because a first novel is heavily autobiographical and the writer has spent years on it. If it is successful, the publisher may press for a follow-up novel to be produced quickly, sometimes with a sacrifice in quality. Therefore it's natural for first-time novelists to worry about whether their second effort will live up to their initial work, but in some cases writers start worrying about this before they've even *finished* the first one.

There are two answers to this anxiety. Some authors only ever produce one work. The prime example is Harper Lee, with her masterpiece *To Kill a Mockingbird*. Not only has this book given pleasure to millions, it has also had an important social impact. When the civil rights lawyers who risked their lives in the 1960s and early 1970s in pursuit of equal rights for black people were asked what inspired them to do this, many of them named *To Kill a Mockingbird* as one of the influences. If you were to write only a single book but it had the power of that one, would that be so bad?

Realistically, however, most authors have many books in them. One way to reassure yourself of this is to keep a notebook of ideas for future books while you're writing the first one. Jot down any and all ideas for stories, characters, settings, situations, bits of dialogue, etc. Don't let them distract you from putting most of your energy into your current book, but keep your notebook handy as a reminder that ideas are plentiful. Chapter 4, "An Endless Flow of Ideas," will also give you strategies for generating even more ideas when you need them.

The fear that you're too old

There's so much emphasis these days on young and attractive writers that you may fear you're not the right type for today's publishing scene. Publishers do rejoice when they find an author who can look sexy on the back cover and be promoted as the next young discovery. However, there are always exceptions. In 2003, the winner of the Whitbread Award was Norman Lebrecht, age 54, for his novel *The Song of Names*. In the *Guardian* newspaper he said, "Here there are agents who are prepared to put their faith in someone who is on the wrong side of 50." Others who started late and thrived include Annie Proulx, Penelope Fitzgerald, and Mary Wesley.

Lebrecht makes the case for mature writers:

> *"When I read a novel, I like to hear the voice of someone who has experience. There are many art forms that are particularly suited to young people, in which young people can have their say—there's pop music, there's theatre—much better suited to the very young than to the middle-aged. But the*

novel and the symphony are contemplative forms, into which you try to pack as much of what you know about life as possible, as much as you never even knew you knew."

The fear of being overwhelmed by research

If you are writing a historical novel, or a book set in another part of the world, or in a specialized field, you may worry you'll never be able to get all the details right. Numerous projects have been abandoned when the author was drawn deeper and deeper into research, until it turned into a maze from which there seemed to be no exit.

Giles Minton is a journalist who wrote the non-fiction book *Samurai William*, about the first Englishman to visit Japan. In *Writers' News* he said:

> *"It's very different writing 100,000 words when you have been used to doing 1,000 or 2,000 words. I think the one thing that journalism has taught me is that structure is all-important. I did quite a bit of reading before I started* Samurai William *so I had the general, overall view of the book, and then I had to break it down into chapters. Then you can break down chapters into segments. I think when you are dealing with such massive amounts of information you have to control it."*

Minton's method offers hope to those who fear handling large amount of research:

> *"I have the overview of the book and I tend to research a chapter and then write a chapter. There is so much information involved that I couldn't possibly research the whole book first."*

The internet is of course a fantastic resource for researchers. It can locate not only facts, but also friendly experts willing to answer questions or look over sections of the book about which you are unsure. You may be surprised at how flattered experts are when someone asks them to review a book for accuracy; many will do it for free, others for a reasonable fee. The possibilities offered by the internet offer another reason not to let research frighten you.

And a word about courage...

In his wonderful book *The Courage to Create*, Rollo May wrote:

> *"If you do not express your own original ideas, if you do not listen to your own being, you will have betrayed yourself. Also you will have betrayed our community in failing to make your contribution to the whole."*

That's what writing is all about. If you still have fears, put them aside now and focus your attention and your energy on what only you can write. The rest of this book will help you find the resources and techniques for making your contribution. The result may be an article, a story, a book, or a script that will feed the imagination and the dreams of people you'll never meet, whose names you'll never know, but with whom you will have communicated because you had the courage to follow your dream.

KEY POINTS

- The biggest obstacle to writing success is usually yourself.
- Some people let their fears stop them from writing. The seven big fears are:
  - The fear of rejection
  - The fear that it won't be good enough
  - The fear of success

- •➤ The fear of revealing too much
- •➤ The fear that you have only one book in you
- •➤ The fear that you are too old
- •➤ The fear of being overwhelmed by research
- ✐ All of these fears can be overcome, as described in this chapter.

EXERCISES

- ✐ If you suffer from any of the seven fears, challenge them every morning.
- ✐ As you read about the success of other writers, jot down how their experience disproved the fears that you worry about.

CHAPTER BONUS

On the website www.yourwritingcoach.com, click on the "Chapter Bonuses" tab, then the "No More Fears" tab, and type in the code: nofear. You will be taken to an exclusive interview with journalist and documentary maker Lucy Jago, who overcame her fear of writing a full-length book and produced *The Northern Lights*, which won her the Andrew Lownie Biographer's Club Prize and a six-figure deal with a major publisher.

2

Find Your Niche

"Make visible what, without you, might never have been seen."

—*Robert Bresson*

You have the impulse to write, but maybe you're not sure yet exactly *what* you want to write. It's not unusual for creative people to try to do everything, preferably all at the same time. If you want to make writing a hobby, then by all means jump around and write as many different things as you like. But if you aim to be a professional writer, it makes sense to focus on one type of writing and work hard to gain expertise and success in that arena.

The easiest way to figure out what you should write is to answer this question: What do you love to read? If you devour mysteries, or haunt the bookshop waiting for the latest Stephen King and Clive Barker novels, or you have a bookshelf full of science fiction, there's your answer. Even within a category such as "crime," there are many sub-categories, such as traditional mysteries, police procedurals (with another sub-category of forensics), comic crime, and so on. The more specific you can be the better, because agents and publishers will need to know where your book fits.

Write what you are passionate about, not what you think will sell. If you are trying to write in a genre that doesn't really speak to you, the results will reflect that. When J.K. Rowling became immensely wealthy after creating Harry Potter, thousands of would-be writers decided they would also write about boy wizards, but the successful similar books came from authors who were already in love with the fantasy genre before it became a big money-spinner.

My advice is the same for those who want to write non-fiction: Be guided by what you love to read, not by the fact that Civil War books or cookbooks or books on relationships are hot at the moment.

At the same time, it's important to be aware of the general trends in book publishing, newspapers, television, and magazines. If a format or genre is totally out of fashion, it would be an uphill battle to try to revive it single-handedly. For example, when I was growing up there were at least a dozen Western series on American prime-time network television, but that genre has been out of favor for years. Similarly, romance novels used to mean a chaste young lady falling for a slick stranger only to discover in the end that life with the boy next door is her true destiny, and the story ended with nothing more explicit than a kiss. While that formula still exists, it is now the exception rather than the rule. In the magazine world, the market for short stories has almost disappeared, and articles typically are much shorter than they used to be. If you write in the genres you read, you'll be aware of what's happening in your segment of the publishing or television and film world.

Even once you have narrowed down your choice between fiction and non-fiction, if you want to write fiction you still have to decide whether to focus on short stories or novels or scripts or plays or poems. If you want to write non-fiction, you have to choose between books and articles. If you already know what you want to write, you can skip the rest of this chapter. If not, to help you decide, I'll sum up the key aspects of each major type of writing.

Writing novels

Writing a novel is a long-term commitment. Leaving aside the quality for a moment, the sheer quantity of words can be intimidating. Novels vary greatly in length, but a typical first novel runs at about 75,000 words. On the plus side, this gives you a great canvas on which to create your story, and plenty of time to go deeply into the characters. You can span generations if you like, and one of the joys of a novel is that you may come to look forward to spending lots of time with the people you have created.

With this comes the challenge of finding a set of characters, a plot, and a structure that will maintain the reader's interest for that long. Many an attempted novel has petered out after the first hundred pages when the author realized that he or she had used up all of the story. This is especially scary for writers who don't like to outline or plan their story too far ahead. Therefore it's worth thinking carefully before you start whether you have chosen a theme and a situation that can sustain a long narrative.

Novel writers have to be good at all the aspects of fiction writing: dialogue, descriptions, action. If you don't enjoy writing descriptions but love to write dialogue, you might be happier writing plays or screenplays.

Although the media play up the handful of authors who have become rich from their bestsellers, the typical novelist's experience is different. The advance for a first novel averages around $5,000 (£2,500). This advance is yours to keep no matter what, and if the royalties on your book add up to more than the advance, you get the extra. Of course, every writer hopes that his or her novel will be the one that catches the attention of the critics, or is mentioned on the *Richard and Judy* television show in the UK or on *Oprah*, and shoots to the top of the bestseller charts. It happened for one of my workshop participants, Lucy Jago, and every time I send one of my own new projects into the world, it's with the hope that it will do well. However, I suggest that you don't expect to get rich from writing novels.

Even once you have sold your novel to a publisher, your work is not done. These days, as we'll see in more detail in Chapters 15 and 16, the writer is increasingly responsible for marketing his or her book. This entails radio and television talk shows, talks to groups, book signings, and so forth. If you are terminally shy, this might prove to be strenuous for you; on the other hand, since it'll be your baby that you're pushing, you may surprise yourself and find you enjoy it. And there's nothing that quite matches the fun of spotting someone reading your book!

To sum it up, if you want to tell big stories (or small stories in great detail), if you love the challenge of mastering all the elements of writing, and if you have stamina and determination, you're well suited to writing novels.

Writing screenplays

Writing your first screenplay is also a solitary experience. This will be a "spec" script, meaning you are writing it on speculation, not on commission. Generally, no one will want to commission you to create a script until they have seen evidence that you can write one. The spec script is your calling card. It may sell and, sometimes more importantly, it may impress producers enough that they ask you to adapt a novel or write another script for them.

Scriptwriting is especially enjoyable for those who love to write dialogue. Although you will be describing the action, too, it will be in very concise ways. For instance, in a script you might write, "George walks into the bar. The décor hasn't changed much since the 1930s." If the film is made, the set designer will be the one who has to decide exactly how the bar will look, the props that might be used, and so forth. By contrast, a novelist might spend a few paragraphs describing the location in some detail.

Scriptwriters have to follow a specific format and their scripts must be a fixed length for television slots and between about 95 and 125 pages for feature films. Some writers like having a fixed length to work to, others find it frustrating.

Once you have sold the script or started working on commissioned scripts, the experience of a scriptwriter differs drastically from that of a novelist. At that point, you have no further right to determine or influence your work's fate. It may be that you wrote a wonderfully gentle coming-of-age story, but if the studio decides it should be changed to a lurid tale of the decline and fall of a young prostitute, they can make that change without your permission.

In Hollywood, just about every film that gets released has had a succession of writers, or more accurately rewriters, working on it. You don't see all their names on the credits, because the Writers Guild limits the number of writers who can be credited and the bias is strongly in favor of the original writer(s). Sometimes this kind of rewriting ruins your work, other times it makes it better. In the UK and the rest of Europe, there is more respect for the role of the writer, but no guarantees that your opinions will be heeded. This relative lack of power led to the classic joke about the starlet who was so dumb that in an effort to get ahead, she slept with a writer.

I don't want to paint too negative a picture, however. When my film *The Real Howard Spitz* was made, director Vadim Jean consulted me about any changes he wanted, and I did all the rewrites myself. I even got to appear in a scene with the star of the film, Kelsey Grammer. I also had very positive experiences on the TV movies I wrote for the Olsen twins, with producer Jim Green. My point is that if you are a control freak or thin-skinned, you probably shouldn't be writing scripts. If you are flexible, diplomatic, patient, and open to suggestion, you have the right personality for this type of writing.

There's good news on the money front. Scriptwriters, especially those who write feature films, are routinely better paid than any other kind of writer. Writers Guild minimum fees have been established for most kinds of scripts and experienced writers are paid more than the minimum. However, not all production companies are signatories to the Writers Guild agreements, so you may also be offered less. If someone commissions you to write a script, typically you will be offered a "step deal," which means that you will get an agreed amount for each step of the process. The steps might be first an outline, then a first draft, then a second draft, then a polish. If the buyer is very unhappy with what you deliver at any stage, he or she can fire you and then you will not be entitled to the fees that go with the rest of the steps. However, if you're writing scripts, most likely you will have an agent to look out for your interests (for information on what agents do and how to get one, see Chapter 15).

Writing for the theater

Writing for the theater has some elements in common with writing scripts, but of course you are limited to what can happen on a stage. With clever scenery and effects this need not necessarily be a problem, as proven by the fact that there has been a stage production of *Lord of the Rings*, and that the musical *Starlight Express* features people (representing different kinds of trains) whizzing around the theater on roller skates. If you and the director, set designer, and actors have done your jobs well, the audience will accept just about any reality you give them.

The productions that are in the spotlight are those in London's West End and on Broadway, but those are extremely tough markets to crack, especially since musicals have taken over so many of the theaters. But there's a hidden market that absorbs a lot of plays, and that's amateur and local theater. Thousands of productions are staged every year in schools, church halls, small theaters, and other venues. They are looking for plays with certain characteristics: large casts so that everybody can have a role, more women than men (because more women and girls are willing to take part than men and boys), and material that is not controversial. There is a demand for one-act plays as well as full-length works with these qualities. While this may limit you in some ways, it's a good market and not as competitive as many of the others.

In most instances, you would be paid a small advance and then royalties, which are also small but can add up. I have a one-act play circulating in this market and every year I get a notice of royalties, which also reveals where it has been produced. I find it fun to see the names of some pretty obscure towns where some group or other has seen fit to stage my work. To actually make a living from this market you have to write a lot of plays, but once you get a few making the rounds, the royalties can give you a nice supplemental income. The website www.yourwritingcoach.com lists books that will guide you regarding how and where to submit plays.

Writing children's books

Harry Potter has a lot to answer for. Publishers have reported being inundated by queries and submissions from people who have suddenly decided they want to write books for young people. Children's books have always been a difficult market because they look easy to write. This is especially true of picture books: a hundred words or so, and you're done! Yes, it's only a hundred words, but it has to be the *right* hundred words.

People who tell their children or grandchildren bedtime stories about how Clever Mousekin outwits Mr. Cat sometimes think this qualifies them to write a successful children's book. Of course, it's important to relate well to children, but it's equally important to study what is already available. Some people are surprised by the sophistication of a lot of children's literature, and the variety of topics with which it deals. There is still a demand for escapist tales, but there is also a strong market for books that help children to understand the less sunny aspects of life.

If it's a picture book you want to write, you don't need to create the pictures yourself or find an artist to do them, that will be the publisher's responsibility. However, you should give a brief description of the visuals you think could go on each page.

If writing for children—not *down to* children—is something you can do, you will have a good chance of success despite the competitiveness of this market.

Writing short stories and poetry

Short stories tend to be about a moment in time, or one part of a character's life, or a tale with a twist. They require less of a time commitment and can range from one page to 30 or 40 pages in length. Like novels, you need to have the skill to write both description and dialogue, but the plotting requirements are less daunting. That's not to say that writing an excellent short story is easy, just that it demands less stamina on the part of both the writer and the reader.

Unfortunately, the market for short stories has been shrinking for decades. Most consumer magazines and even quite a few newspapers used to feature short stories. Now very few do, and the short story lives on primarily in small press publications. Some of these focus on one genre, such as horror or science fiction, others specialize in more literary short fiction. Most of the short story collections that come out in book form are written by authors who have already made their names as novelists. Therefore, writing short stories is not going to earn you a lot of money, but it offers tremendous creative freedom, and many successful novelists credit their experience in writing short stories with giving them the skills and confidence to proceed to the longer form.

Poetry also is confined to specialist publications and collections these days. Poets have never expected to make much money, but theirs is possibly the most personal of the writing arts, and getting published even in a small-circulation magazine can be satisfying. There are also poetry websites on which poets can share their work. If you go to Google or another search engine and enter the key words "poetry sites," you will find them.

Writing non-fiction books

Far more non-fiction books are published than novels. The subjects of such books cover a tremendous range, and the demand for personal development and "how-to" topics has increased over the past few years. Naturally, publishers will expect that you have special expertise or experience in the area you want to write about. This doesn't mean you have to have formal qualifications, though; relevant life experience can qualify. Most important is finding a fresh angle on the topic.

For British chef Jamie Oliver, this took two forms. One is that his approach to cooking emphasized simple, wholesome food, and it came at a time when people were getting tired of the snobbish approach to cuisine. The other was the title of his first book and television show, *The Naked Chef* (referring to the cooking, not the cook!). It was provocative enough to capture people's attention and different enough to be memorable. Both of these were congruent with Oliver's sunny, upbeat disposition, and certainly his likability (which may now have diminished somewhat due to overexposure) was also a factor.

The one area I would warn most people away from is the memoir. Unless you have been in the public eye or have a truly remarkable experience to relate, it is difficult to interest people outside of your immediate family in your life story (sometimes it's even hard to interest people inside your family...). Of course, you have the option of self-publishing such a work and distributing it to friends and relatives.

One of the advantages of writing non-fiction is that you don't need to write the whole book in order to find out whether publishers are interested. All you need is a proposal and a couple of sample chapters. In Chapter 15 you'll see what goes into a book proposal and how to write one. You or your agent can send the proposal to a number of publishers. If they are interested, they will either ask to see more, or immediately offer you a contract to finish the book.

The amount of money made by writers of non-fiction books varies widely, of course. Unless yours is a very hot topic, especially one that creates a bidding war between several publishers, your advance is likely to be modest, between $4,000 and $10,000 (£2–5,000). You will then receive royalties as soon as that advance has been earned out. Books on a specialized topic are unlikely to hit the bestseller lists, but they can give you a steady income over time.

For example, the book I co-wrote with my friend Kerry Cox, *Successful Scriptwriting*, went out of print recently after almost 20 years on the market, having sold about 65,000 copies. There is also the potential for income from foreign editions. My book *Do Something Different*, published in the UK by Virgin Books, has also come out in Chinese, Korean, Spanish, and Bulgarian editions. The royalties from foreign versions of a book typically are not huge, but they all add up.

Writing articles

The market for articles is healthy. Most magazines use at least a few freelance writers, and some are written almost entirely by material from freelancers. The topics span a huge range, as a look at the tremendous variety of magazines available will show. It's a good idea to specialize in one area, so that editors get to know you and trust your expertise. Even if you are not an expert yourself, you can create articles that quote others who are.

A handful of publications pay very well indeed for articles, but in most instances the fees are relatively modest. If you can supply photos to go with the written material, that will make the article more appealing and you'll be paid an additional fee for the pictures. To make a living writing pieces demands that you write a lot of them, but skillful article writers often find a way to sell three or four different ones all drawing on the same research. For example, let's say you do an interview with a local man who has won prizes for growing roses. You could sell one version to a gardening magazine, another to his local newspaper with a "neighborhood man makes good" angle, and another to a magazine for retired people on how he came to take up this hobby later in life.

If you have lots of ideas for articles, feel comfortable interviewing people either in person or on the phone, and are organized enough to keep track of your query letters, submissions, and invoices, you're an excellent candidate for writing articles.

Decision time

I hope now you have a better idea of what kind of writing appeals to you most. Over the course of your writing career you can write many different kinds of things. Some novelists get a chance to adapt their book for the stage or screen, and some people write lots of articles and then eventually a book on the same subject. What is important is to pick one arena and get started.

KEY POINTS

- The easiest way to figure out what you should write is to consider what you love to read.
- Writing novels requires endurance and all-around skills, as well as the willingness and ability to help market your book.
- Writing screenplays is lucrative, but when the script sells you lose creative control and your work may be changed.
- Writing for the theater requires particular skill with dialogue, and the largest market is for plays aimed at the amateur and schools markets.
- Writing children's books requires you to relate well to children's tastes and to study the market.
- Writing short stories gives you a lot of creative freedom, but the commercial demand for them is shrinking.
- Writing non-fiction books requires that you have some specific expertise or are able to research well, but it is a huge market.
- Writing articles requires you to be prolific, but it also is a healthy market.

EXERCISES

- When you have decided which type of writing to focus on, stop being just a consumer and become an analyst. If something you read works, break it down to see why and how it works, and do the same with books or scripts or stories that don't work to see *why* they don't.
- If you find yourself tempted to jump around between genres, keep a notebook in which you can jot down all of your ideas so they won't be lost, but stay with the current genre until you have completed and marketed at least one project.

CHAPTER BONUS

On the website www.yourwritingcoach.com, click on the "Chapter Bonuses" tab, then the "Find Your Niche" tab, and type in the code: niche. You will be taken to an exclusive interview with Peter Guttridge, who is the crime fiction critic for the *Observer* newspaper and the author of six comic crime novels, on what makes a good crime story.

3

Use Your Special Knowledge

"We don't know who we are until we see what we can do."
—*Martha Grimes*

Maybe you've heard the old adage, "Write what you know." Naturally, this isn't a strict rule, otherwise there would be no fantasy or science fiction novels, and serial killer thrillers could be written only by serial killers. But if you have special knowledge and experience that you can work into your fiction or nonfiction project, that is a definite advantage, in terms of providing interesting content and increased credibility with publishers and the public. This applies to just about anybody: people in advertising, finance, education, public relations, even homemakers who can convey their experience with a unique style or angle.

What do you know?

Even if you haven't worked in any particularly interesting fields, don't assume that means you lack material to draw on. Take a moment to review what you've experienced and learned from:

- your experiences and relationships growing up
- the places you have lived
- the friends you have had
- your hobbies
- your time in school
- the jobs you've held
- any volunteer work you've done

- the places you've visited
- your romantic relationships
- your experiences as a parent or aunt, uncle, or godparent

In this chapter I'm going to focus on three areas that are particularly hot: police, medical, and legal. Even if you haven't participated in these three worlds, however, read on and think about how you could apply the same techniques and principles to the field you know most about. Let's start by meeting some practitioners in each of these areas and hear what they say about their approaches to writing.

Crime does pay

The umbrella of crime writing covers several categories. In recent years, one of the hottest has been novels, films, and television series dealing with forensics. A bestselling novelist working in this sub-genre is Kathy Reichs, whose books include *Break No Bones* and *Cross Bones*. She is a forensic anthropologist for the authorities in North Carolina and Quebec Province. Her first experience working in forensic labs was in Montreal, trying to help identify the bones found in a wooded area where a child had gone missing several months before. She was able to establish that the death was a homicide. In an interview on her website (www.kathy reichs.com), she sums up the attraction of her kind of writing:

> *"What's appealing about the modern murder mystery, the type of thing that I write or the profiling, is bringing science to bear on these questions, rather than the intuitive approach that might have been more typical of some of the earlier, and some modern, mystery writers. I think we bring science to the question of 'who done it.'"*

Colin Campbell, a British author who retired after 30 years as a police officer, writes more traditional police thrillers, such as *The*

Ballad of the One-Legged Man. He says that as well as dealing with a specific crime, it is about "the importance of friendship on the front lines and how much more painful betrayal is because of that." This illustrates the fact that readers are interested not only in the procedures of police work, but also in the way it affects police officers' private lives, and the kinds of moral and ethical dilemmas they face. Campbell likes to fill what he considers an underserved niche. He told *Spinetingler* magazine:

> *"The police elements are all based on real jobs I dealt with or knew about. Happy or sad, it's all there. The gallows humour just helps you through the shift. And the cameraderie. There doesn't seem to be anyone writing about the front line copper in uniform. Not detective superintendents chasing serial killers but the real nitty-gritty, in the trenches stuff. Not since Joseph Wambaugh's* The Choirboys *in America. I like to think my crime books, so far, are a tribute to the boys in blue."*

Some law enforcement personnel, such as John Douglas, also write non-fiction crime books. Douglas worked as a profiler for the FBI until 1995, pursuing predators like the Atlanta child murderer and Seattle's Green River Killer. He styles himself the "Mindhunter," and his books include the true crime tale *Anyone You Want Me to Be*, the story of the internet's first serial killer. Douglas's website, www.johndouglasmindhunter.com, features some fascinating articles on the work of profilers. This is one author who takes merchandising seriously: From his site, you can buy John Douglas "Mindhunter" caps, coffee mugs, caps, bumper stickers, and mouse pads.

The doctors are in

Since 1985, Jonathan Kellerman has written more than 20 novels, including a long series featuring psychologist Alex Delaware.

Kellerman told *The New York Times* that for 14 years he was a failed writer, while getting his PhD in psychology, a medical school professorship, and a job at a pediatric hospital, specializing in childhood trauma. Looking back, he says he wrote, but didn't rewrite, "assiduously neglecting the basics of story structure." He also didn't let his experience truly inform his writing:

> *"I was afraid of revealing anything about myself and conjured tales that bore no semblance to my reality or anyone else's."*

When he was ready to get more personal, he created Alex Delaware, who, Kellerman says, "emerged braver, thinner and better looking than I was." He teamed Delaware with a police officer, who, trying to avoid clichés, he made a gay homicide detective. That book, *When the Bough Breaks*, won two major awards and became a word-of-mouth bestseller. Kellerman says:

> *"As a psychologist I attempted to construct rules about human behavior. As a novelist I'm obsessed by the exceptions."*

Probably the best-known contemporary writer to exploit his medical background is Michael Crichton. After graduating from Harvard Medical School, he wrote such novels as *The Andromeda Strain*, *Timeline*, and *State of Fear*. His books have sold over 100 million copies and he also created the television series *ER*. He is the only person to have had, at the same time, the number one book, the number one movie, and the number one television show in the United States. I'm beginning to hate him...

Seriously, one of his many talents is to be in touch with the issues that people are thinking and talking about, especially in the arenas of medicine and science, and then to wrap those up in compelling plots that keep us on the edge of our seats. Sometimes he has been ahead of the times. He wrote a film version of *ER* as early as 1974, but nobody wanted to make the movie. Producers thought it was too technical, chaotic, and fast-moving. As he writes on his website, www.crichton-official.com:

> "*It sat on a shelf for the next nineteen years—brought out every five or ten years, for updating, and for the studios and networks to look at, and reject yet again. Finally NBC made it as a TV pilot. And it became a series.*"

That's a bit of an understatement: *ER* has been the winner of 22 Emmy Awards including Outstanding Drama Series (1996), with an industry record 115 nominations.

It's the law

The foremost writer of legal-related fiction these days is John Grisham. After graduating from law school at the University of Mississippi, he practiced law for nearly ten years, specializing in criminal defense and personal injury litigation. It was over-hearing the story of a child rape victim that gave him the idea to write a novel exploring what might have happened if such a victim's father murdered her attackers. That book was *A Time to Kill*, published in 1987 to modest sales (the entire edition was only 5,000 books). Grisham was already working on his next book, *The Firm*. When Paramount paid $600,000 for the film rights Doubleday bought the book, and *The Firm* became the bestselling novel of 1991. Grisham went on to write *The Pelican Brief* and *The Client*, also bestsellers, after which *A Time to Kill* was republished and this time around was also a huge hit. Worldwide, more than 60 million of his books are in print.

Grisham tends to be a private man, but he answered some email questions for *The Book Report* a few years ago. He said the most satisfying thing about the law was "getting out of it." He revealed that he used to wake up at 5 a.m. for three years to spend an hour or so each morning writing before going to work. Now his routine has changed:

"I write six months a year. I find my story, find its voice, its people, its pace, and I retreat into my attic for six hours a day and shut out everything but family. As I write, I don't think about the readers, the sales, the movies. I think about the story. If I get it right, everything else falls into place."

It's interesting that although lawyers don't evoke much respect from the public, there is always a demand for novels set in the legal world. The clue as to why may lie in Grisham's books, many of which have a David-vs.-Goliath theme. An ordinary individual (who generally is a lawyer) takes on the system, which may be a big corporation or law firm, and triumphs.

Ron Sharrow is the author of *The Sword of Justice*, subtitled *A Lawyer's Revenge*. It was his first book, although he has another one, *Conspiracy*, to be published shortly. I caught up with him at a book signing and asked him how he came to start writing novels. This is what he said:

"I practiced law in Baltimore for 38 years, and during the early years of my practice I did a lot of criminal work. Throughout all the years of my practice I kept a journal of all the stupid things people said and did, the crazy situations they got themselves involved in, very funny stuff—funnier than fiction. I kept that journal so I wouldn't forget, not with any intent of writing anything. When I retired, about nine years ago, I was going through that journal and I thought, 'This stuff is priceless, it really should be shared.' So I created a character, C. Bruce West, a young, energetic lawyer who is very successful in his practice but has a totally screwed-up personal life, and he's relating to the reader many of these stories about the things that happened to him during the course of his daily activities, and some of the more bizarre criminal cases he was involved in. It's not an autobiographical book, but it's inspired by those stories that were real. It's fictionalized accounts of those, written to be humorous and also with some suspense. It's the first of a series; I've written

four C. Bruce West books, each with some relationship to the others, but also able to stand on their own."

If you've kept a journal, even one that is more personal in nature, you probably have a gold mine of experiences to draw on. And if you don't keep a journal, maybe now is a good time to start.

The problem of ethics

When I was writing television films, there were three categories of what were called docu-dramas: "a true story," which meant that we had acquired all the rights to an actual case, including contracts with all the principal real-life characters; "based on a true story," which generally meant that we had made a deal with one or two of the main players, and based the rest on public records; and "inspired by a true story," which meant that the work had very little relationship to the real story, but we hoped that label would attract more viewers than a film classified as pure fiction.

Police officers, doctors, and lawyers all face ethical and legal issues when they are basing their fiction on real events. That's why most of them are happy to be inspired by actual cases, but go on to fictionalize the story enough that nobody will sue them. Some of them regard this need as an asset. Jonathan Kellerman says:

> *"Too much reliance upon reality stiffens and cripples fiction... Professional ethics forced me to imagine, and that made me a better writer."*

Ron Sharrow comments:

> *"I changed names, I changed places, dates, but in reality the things that people say actually were said to me, maybe not always in the same vein. The criminal cases themselves are a matter of public record and were real cases that were tried."*

True-crime writers tend to rely on widely reported information, court records, and interviews with the people involved. In the case of interviews, it's always important to get a release form that states that the person is happy to allow you to quote them. Some lawyers recommend that you pay the person a token fee, even just £1, as a way to substantiate that you and they entered into a contract.

I don't have the space to go into this in detail, but for good information on such legal matters in the UK a useful book is *Writer's Guide to Copyright and Law*, published by How To Books. For those in the US, a helpful site is www.starvingartistslaw.com.

Use your expertise, but don't overuse it

All of the authors I have cited bring their professional experience into their writing, but they don't let it become overwhelming. Readers and viewers welcome a look behind the scenes of police work, medicine, and the law (or any other specialist field), but they don't want that at the expense of a good story, good dialogue, good characters, and all the other hallmarks of good fiction. For example, *ER* is full of medical jargon sprayed out at a furious pace, but it's the emotional, human stories that make the series compelling. The medical terminology just helps to convince viewers that they are in a high-pressure, life-and-death setting.

The best strategy is to use your specialized knowledge to sprinkle in interesting facts that wouldn't otherwise be known, to create a sense of realism for the settings and the characters, and to let people feel they're right in the middle of your world.

If you can combine that with the techniques of skillful writing covered in the coming chapters, you'll have the formula for a winning book, story, or screenplay.

Your expertise is a marketing asset

When agents, publishers, and producers look at a manuscript or a script, one of the questions in the back of their minds is, "What qualifies this writer to write about this topic?" If two people have written equally good murder mysteries set in a monastery, and one researched monastery life really carefully and the other actually was a monk for 20 years, which one do you think the buyer will go for? Of course it will be the ex-monk, not only because his knowledge will be first-hand but also because it will be easier to get radio, television, and print reporters interested in interviewing him. Personal experience is always a great publicity and marketing angle. However, don't despair if you don't have this kind of experience; in Chapter 16 you'll discover many other ways of getting attention for your writing.

KEY POINTS

- Novels, screenplays, and non-fiction books by authors who have specialized experience or knowledge have an advantage.
- All facets of your life experience can be drawn on to create interesting stories.
- There is particular interest in books written by police officers, doctors, and lawyers (assuming they are well written).
- In works of fiction based on real cases, care must be taken not to cross the line in terms of ethics and legality.
- Information about these special worlds can help the reader or viewer to feel like an insider, but must not be allowed to overwhelm the story or slow down its pace.
- Personal experience is an asset in marketing your writing.

EXERCISES

- Take some time to go over everything you have experienced so that you don't underestimate the resource that your life represents.
- If you're already familiar with the main authors in your particular domain, make a point of also reading some who write about other specific realms. See whether anything they do especially well can be applied to writing about your arena.
- If you're not quite ready to tackle a novel or non-fiction book in your area of specialization, consider starting with some short stories or articles.

CHAPTER BONUS

On the website www.yourwritingcoach.com, click on the "Chapter Bonuses" tab, then the "Knowledge" tab, and type in the code: knowledge. You will be taken to an exclusive interview with Michael Ridpath, who has written eight novels, many of them bestsellers, that draw on his knowledge of banking, trading, and venture capital.

PART II
WRITE!

"Vision without execution is a hallucination."
—*Thomas Edison*

Now that you've decided what to write, let's get right to it! In this section, you find out how to come up with an endless flow of ideas for whatever you write, and how to use the magic question "Why?" to create a blueprint for your writing project. Naturally, you want your characters (real or fictional) to come alive on the page, so there is a chapter about how to do that organically. Next, you find the story secrets that will help make your readers turn those pages. Of course, how you use the language is part of what will set your writing apart, so we look at how to make your prose compelling. And because nobody gets it totally right in the first draft, there's a chapter that shows you how to make fast and easy work of rewriting.

4

An Endless Flow of Ideas

"You can't wait for inspiration. You have to go after it with a club."

—Jack London

Inspiration is wonderful, when it happens. The problem is that it is notoriously unreliable. In this chapter you will discover strategies and techniques to help you come up with ideas whenever you need them.

I first became interested in this area when I started writing for television. My agent set up appointments for me to pitch ideas to various series. At each meeting I was expected to present six to eight storylines that suited that show. I quickly realized it would be very helpful to have a method for coming up with good concepts, rather than sitting around and hoping some would occur to me randomly. Over the years I have continued to research and develop new approaches for generating ideas, and here I will share the best ones with you.

Before we start, let's consider some simple guidelines to keep in mind for effective brainstorming.

The four brainstorming guidelines

1   *Go for quantity.* Try to come up with as many ideas as possible, as quickly as possible.
2   *No judging!* Later you will evaluate all the ideas you have come up with, but if you do that while generating ideas you stop the flow.

3   *Write everything down.* Not writing something down is a
    form of judging it, so capture every idea, no matter how
    crazy or off topic it may seem.
4   *Build on other ideas.* Don't get hung up on trying to develop
    something completely new, because in reality there is almost
    nothing totally new in the world. Even the most amazing
    breakthroughs tend to be combinations of existing
    elements.

Of these four guidelines, the hardest by far to observe is the second. We seem to be trained to judge every idea instantly, and
usually to judge it harshly. If you brainstorm in pairs or a group,
remind each other not to judge—not even with a look or an
intonation, or a self-deprecating comment like "This probably
isn't a very good idea, but…" If you have a particular problem
with doing this, you probably have an out-of-control inner critic,
and Chapter 12 will help you transform it into a more constructive inner guide.

You may want to jot down the four guidelines on a sticky note
and put that on a wall somewhere near your desk. Now you're
ready to let the ideas flow. One way is to apply a question that is
so helpful that using it is akin to creativity magic.

Asking "What if...?" and other questions

Questions are a writer's best friends, for they open the door to an
almost unlimited treasure trove of subject matter. That's true for
fiction and non-fiction. One good question to start with is "What
if…?" What if a female police officer spent five nights a week
patrolling the toughest part of the city? What kinds of problems
would she run into? What kind of attitudes would she encounter
from the denizens of those mean streets? How would the male
police officers respond to her? In the answers to these questions
there lurks a newspaper or magazine article, a short story, a script
for a television program, feature film, or play, a non-fiction book,

a novel, even a poem. How much reality you want to use and how much imagination depends on what you're writing (as we've seen in the last decade or so, if you use too much imagination in your newspaper articles, they make you give back your Pulitzer).

To make the most of the "What if...?" question, you have to let your mind run free. First, generate some subjects. Pick up a newspaper and leaf through it. Jot down the topics of 10 or 20 stories. For example, here are a few from a newspaper I have in front of me: rat infestation discovered at local shopping mall; Eagle Scout honored for saving drowning child; slumlord prosecuted; defective microwaves recalled; first female officer assigned to highest-crime area.

Obviously you don't want to write on the exact subject you've just read about, somebody's already done that. But you can use these topics as starting points. Put yourself in a state of curiosity and jot down all the questions that occur to you. If your mind wanders to other ideas, don't fight it, jot those down, too. Also, don't worry about which (if any) of the questions you will pursue or exactly how the subject fits into the type of project you want to write. All we're doing now is creating raw material; later we will think about how to shape it.

Once you have your list of questions, go over them and consider how answering them might lead to a written piece. For example, as I started to explore earlier, the questions about the female police officer could lead to a "day in the life of" article, or a feature story following a female police cadet through training, or a book of profiles of female police officers in different cities or different countries, or a short story about such an officer's first day on the job, or a film script following a fictional woman from training through to life on the streets.

Let's take another topic: the rat infestation at the shopping mall. What do rats live on? Why have we never been able to eliminate them very effectively? How do exterminators deal with them? Do rats (or their fleas) still carry diseases as they did in the great plagues? If so, why aren't more of us ill? What kinds of people keep rats as pets, and what do they find appealing about them? Again, you have lots of article possibilities: interviews with exterminators, how to prevent rodents infesting your house or apartment, interviews at the pet store with people buying rats for pets, and so on. Or you could write a humorous short story with a persecuted rat as the narrator. There have already been novels and films about rats, so you'd have to find a new way of approaching that topic—we'll look at ways to do that a little later in this chapter.

One more example: the slumlord. What's it really like living in a slum—are the horrors exaggerated? Why don't landlords keep these premises in better condition, or is it the fault of the tenants? Who are the big slumlords in a particular city, and whose job is it to go after them? How effective is law enforcement in this arena, and how severe or minor are the penalties? You could construct an article about a day spent living with a family in these conditions, or an exposé of the slumlords, or an interview with a child psychologist on the effects such living conditions have on children. Or you could write a short story of an incident seen through the eyes of a child living in a slum, or a social worker's doomed attempt to convince a landlord to improve conditions. Or you could create a novel or film script about a slumlord who loses his fortune and has to live the way his former tenants do.

Just by exercising your natural curiosity, you'll be able to generate questions on almost any subject. Then, with your particular type of writing in mind, you can see how those questions can be turned into a written work.

There are several specific "What if…?" questions that can be used to find a fresh angle on a familiar subject.

What if this had happened in a different time period? Again, you can start with the female police officer. Go back in time. Were there female sheriffs or marshals in the Old West? Or female gunfighters? With a little research, you could turn this subject into an interesting feature story for a newspaper or magazine. With a lot of research it might be the foundation of a fascinating novel or screenplay. You could try going further back.

Were there civilizations in which females were responsible for enforcing the law? What about the Amazons? You could also go into the future. In that case, you might write a speculative but fact-based article, for example on the types of technology being developed that decrease the importance of a police officer's sheer physical strength. Or this could lead to a science fiction novel or script about the first female space police officer.

Let's try one more of the sample topics, namely the landlord being fined for allowing slum conditions. Going back in time, have slums always been a feature of cities? Again, research might result in an article comparing the slums of ancient Rome to those of today, or to a book covering the history of slums. Or it might lead to a novel narrated by a boy who grew up in the slums at the turn of the twentieth century and whose determination to make a better life spurred him to become one of the most powerful men in Europe.

What if the story took place in a different location? With the police officer, we have already considered having the action occur in the Old West or in outer space. You might also find out the extent to which other countries use female law enforcement officers. For the rats, what if the infestation took place on an ocean liner instead of a shopping mall? Further, let's assume that the rats are carrying a deadly disease. There might be a good thriller or screenplay there.

What if the story had ended differently? This question is particularly useful for fiction. In the newspaper story, the Eagle Scout saved the drowning child. What if he hadn't? What if he'd lost his nerve at the last minute and now bears the guilt of knowing he could have saved the child? (All right, I'm borrowing from *Lord Jim*, but Joseph Conrad is dead and there aren't any new ideas anyway.) In fact, the landlord was convicted and fined, but what if he'd been found innocent and a group of his tenants had kidnapped him and forced him to live in his own slum building? Hmm, you might even be able to bring the rats into that story!

Obviously, it's easier to come up with ideas that will sustain short pieces—articles, short stories, or poems—than longer works such as novels, plays, or films. For the latter, your questions probably will give you only a starting point or a general subject that will have to be fleshed out. This is where the magic question "Why?" comes in. It's such a useful question for actually building your story that I have devoted Chapter 5 to it.

Now you have the simple procedure: Start with a subject, generate as many questions as you can, then see what kinds of material could come out of the answers to those questions. The more you exercise your imagination, the easier this process becomes.

Use the power of dreams

One of the most creative things people do is to dream. Think about it for a moment: Each of us creates more than 10,000 little movies, full of action, drama, and excitement, often starring ourselves, our friends, people who are long dead, and sometimes even movie stars. Instantly we write the script, cast the story, direct it, and provide the picture and sound—all without thinking about it. Now that's creativity in action!

There are many cases of writers who took inspiration from dreams. In the summer of 1816, Mary Wollstonecraft Godwin and her future husband, Percy Shelley, visited Lord Byron at his Swiss villa. In the evenings, the guests read ghost stories to each other. One night Byron challenged his guests to write such a story themselves. Mary had what could be called a waking dream. She described it this way:

> "When I placed my head upon my pillow, I did not sleep...
> I saw, with shut eyes but acute mental vision... the pale student of unhallowed arts kneeling beside the things he had put together."

This vision became the basis of her novel *Frankenstein*.

Similarly, Robert Louis Stevenson dreamed the basic idea of his novel *The Strange Case of Dr. Jekyll and Mr. Hyde*, and reported that he was upset when his wife woke him up in the middle of his nightmare.

A more modern master of horror, Stephen King, owes his novel *Misery* to a dream. He told reporter Stan Nicholls:

> *"Like the ideas for some of my other novels, that came to me in a dream. In fact, it happened when I was on Concorde, flying over here, to Brown's [a London hotel]. I fell asleep on the plane, and dreamt about a woman who held a writer prisoner and killed him, skinned him, fed the remains to her pig and bound his novel in human skin. His skin, the writer's skin. I said to myself, 'I have to write this story.'"*

Don't think it's only tales of horror that come up in dreams. Paul McCartney has said that the tune for "Yesterday" came to him in a dream. It happened while the Beatles were filming the movie *Help*. McCartney reported:

> *"I woke up with a lovely tune in my head. I thought, 'That's great, I wonder what that is?' There was an upright piano next to me, to the right of the bed by the window. I got out of bed, sat at the piano, found G, found F sharp minor 7th— and that leads you through then to B to E minor, and finally back to E. It all leads forward logically. I liked the melody a lot, but because I'd dreamed it, I couldn't believe I'd written it. I thought, 'No, I've never written anything like this before.' But I had the tune, which was the most magic thing!"*

The writer who carried his dream work to the greatest extremes was science fiction author A.E. van Vogt. He used to set an alarm clock to go off every 45 minutes. He would wake up, consider how what he'd dreamed in the previous period might advance the story he was writing and try to figure out any story problems, then go back to sleep. This went on all night. It sounds a bit mad, but van Vogt wrote hundreds of short stories and many novels, and was considered one of the top science fiction writers of the mid-twentieth century.

My own experience with dreaming was less dramatic, but still useful. One night as I fell asleep I started to half-dream, half-imagine a grumpy writer of detective novels who goes to see whether his book is still on the shelves at the local bookstore. There he sees the attention a children's book author is getting for a little picture book, and he decides to write kids' books himself. The only problem is that he hates children and has no idea what they'd want to read. I got up and wrote the first six pages of a film script. The next night it happened again, the dream advanced the story, and I wrote the next six pages. I was overjoyed that I had discovered a new way to write a screenplay. I figured if this went on for another 18 nights, I'd have the whole thing written. Of course it never happened again, but I had the beginning of the script of *The Real Howard Spitz*.

By the way, if you think you don't dream, it's highly likely that you just don't remember your dreams. If you put a pen and pad on your bedside table and every morning jot down anything you can from any dreams you recall, your mind will gradually get accustomed to remembering your dreams. Another alternative is to have a small tape recorder handy and speak your dreams into that (this could, however, make you less than popular if you sleep with someone else).

Even if you don't want to try working with your dreams, experiment with devoting the first few minutes after you wake up to producing ideas or solving story problems. In that period, your mind will be making the transition from the dreamy, half-asleep state to being fully awake, and this is a very productive time for having ideas.

Invent the solution

For a problem or challenge, describe a machine that would perfectly solve it. Then figure out how you can, in effect, construct such a machine. For example, let's say you use a prioritized to-do list for your writing-related tasks, but you never actually do them in that order. What you need is a machine that tells you the most important task first, and doesn't tell you the next one until the first is done.

Now brainstorm how you can construct such a machine. One solution would be to make the list and speak the items into a tape recorder in order of priority, leaving a pause between items. Throw away the list and listen to the recorder to hear the first task. Do that, and only then listen for the second one, and so on.

Adapt and adopt

Look around you to see who are the big successes in fields other than yours. Describe as simply as possible what makes them successful. Then brainstorm how one or more of these qualities could be adapted to what you want to do. As an example of success, let's take the Pret a Manger sandwich chain. The elements that have made the company popular include fresh ingredients, fast service, and convenient locations.

Let's assume you'd like to write and sell some newspaper or magazine articles. The equivalent of "fresh ingredients" might be writing about familiar topics (the yo-yo economy, another war in the Middle East, the epidemic of obesity) but with a fresh angle: namely, how each of these affects youngsters or the educational system. The equivalent of "fast service" might be sitting down as soon as a news item comes up on CNN or the BBC, brainstorming related article ideas, and emailing query letters to several editors suggesting a story angle that relates to that development. Most writers would take at least a day or two to do that, but you could do it in a matter of hours. The equivalent of "convenient locations" might be coming up with regional or local slants on news stories to offer to local or regional publications.

Construct an alter ego

When faced with a task you don't enjoy, imagine the kind of person who would enjoy doing it. What qualities would he or she have? How would this person go about doing the task? Then step into that role for the duration.

Let's say you want to get all your papers organized before starting on a major new writing project. Who enjoys doing this? Personally, I imagine a superhero, Anal-Retentive Man, who is focused totally on the task at hand, handles each piece of paper only once, and sees clutter as his arch-enemy. When I imagine him vividly enough and then step into that role, I'm able to sort through papers and old magazines with the drive and determination that normally elude me.

If you are doing exploratory research for a historical novel, you'd want a different alter ego in charge. Maybe Curious Kid. This is a character who wants to know lots of things and is intrigued by strange and interesting facts. In that guise, you could spend quite a few hours reading and researching with no particular goal other than to familiarize yourself with a particular era. However, if you are digging for a specific fact, this would be the wrong persona to use. For that, you might want Dogged Bloodhound as an alter ego, so that you stay on track no matter what the tempting distractions. It's fun to make up your own cast of useful characters and, while it may sound a bit silly, the technique works (and you don't have to tell anybody else you're doing it).

Limber up with the story generator game

If you find that you're having trouble getting your ideas flowing, take a few minutes to play the story generator game. Randomly pick five numbers, each between one and nine. Write them down. Then jot down the elements that correspond to these numbers in the columns overleaf (one from each column).

A: GENRE	B: PERSON	C: SECOND PERSON	D: EMOTION	E: LOCATION
1 Thriller	1 Teacher	1 Baby	1 Jealousy	1 London
2 Comedy	2 Doctor	2 Soldier	2 Greed	2 New York
3 Drama	3 Reporter	3 Nun	3 Love	3 Paris
4 Romantic comedy	4 Parent	4 Priest	4 Fear	4 Delhi
5 Mystery	5 Cop	5 Taxi driver	5 Hate	5 Trinidad
6 Science fiction	6 Child	6 Psychiatrist	6 Revenge	6 Zoo
7 Romance	7 Lawyer	7 Old man	7 Curiosity	7 Countryside
8 Police story	8 Scientist	8 Old woman	8 Lust	8 Old house
9 Horror	9 Nurse	9 Athlete	9 Friendship	9 Prison

Your assignment is to take no more than five minutes to make up a story, or at least the beginnings of a story, putting together those five elements. For example, let's say you randomly choose the numbers 2, 7, 1, 9, and 6 (although it's okay to duplicate numbers). These numbers yield the following elements: A comedy featuring a lawyer and a baby, friendship, and the zoo.

One idea is a comedy in which a lawyer takes her baby to the zoo and strikes up a friendship with a homeless woman who lives there. The lawyer decides to try to improve the homeless woman's life and gets her a job at her law firm, where her fiancé also works. To her horror, it seems like her fiancé is starting to fall in love with the homeless woman.

Now that I put on my evaluator's hat, I don't think that's necessarily a great idea, but I did stick to the five-minute rule and I see some aspects of the story that could work. More importantly, it got my brain warmed up, and that's the main objective of this exercise.

You may have noticed that the one thing all of the preceding techniques have in common is that they are playful. Play is at the heart of creativity, and as soon as you give yourself permission to play, the ideas begin to flow. When you combine that attitude with the practical techniques in this chapter, you will never run out of ideas.

KEY POINTS

- Inspiration is fickle, but there are techniques you can use to generate ideas at will.
- During brainstorming, don't judge the ideas, just generate as many as possible and write them all down.
- Questions, especially "What if…?", open the door to unlimited ideas.
- Dreaming can also be a source of ideas, and you can train yourself to remember your dreams.
- Use successes in other fields to give you ideas to apply to your challenge.
- The alter ego strategy allows you to choose the most useful mental and physical state for the task at hand.
- The story generator game can help you get your imagination moving.

EXERCISES

- Set aside 15 minutes a day, ideally right as you begin to wake up in the mornings, during which to brainstorm. Experiment between directed brainstorming, in which you are trying to solve a problem, and free-form brainstorming, in which you just jot down whatever comes to mind.

- The next time you have trouble achieving a task, create an alter ego who would handle that task better, and do it while in character.
- If you find it hard to get started with a writing session, play the story generator game for five minutes to loosen up your imagination. See whether any of the ideas that come up might be useful somehow in what you are writing at that point.

CHAPTER BONUS

On the website www.yourwritingcoach.com, click on the Chapter Bonuses tab, then the "Ideas" tab, and type in the code: ideas. You will be taken to an exclusive video interview with Roddy Maude-Roxby, actor and master improviser, on how to free up your imagination.

5

The Magic "Why?"

"The ideal way to work on a project is to ask a question you don't know the answer to."

—*Francis Ford Coppola*

In this chapter we will look at how you can use one powerful little word to help you decide what specific project to write and how to write it: "Why?" If you've ever dealt with a young child, you've heard that word a lot. In that case, it probably nearly drove you crazy; in this case, it becomes a valuable writing and motivational tool. It also prepares the way for the chapters that follow, which go deeper into creating characters and structuring your plot.

The first why: Why write this?

Let's start with the most basic question: Why do you want to write the particular project you've chosen? If you have several ideas for writing projects, using the "Why?" technique for all of them can help you decide which one to tackle first.

It couldn't be simpler: Just start (and keep) asking why. First, ask "Why do I want to write this project?" and jot down your answer. For each answer, keep asking why and writing down those answers until you reach a logical stopping point. This could be just two or three questions, or it could be a dozen or more. Here's how it worked for my e-book *Time Management for Writers*:

Q Why do I want to write the book *Time Management for Writers*?

A Because I want to help people who have the desire to write but don't know how to find the time and I think I can do it.

Q Why do I think I can help people who have the desire to write but don't know how to find the time?

A Because I've faced this challenge myself with screen-plays and books and have been frustrated by the traditional approaches to time management.

Q Why have I been frustrated by the traditional approaches to time management?

A Because traditional time management techniques are very mechanical and not geared to creative pursuits.

Q Why are traditional time management techniques not geared to creative pursuits?

A Because they originated in the early part of the twentieth century, when the emphasis was on finding ways to make repetitive tasks more efficient.

That feels like the natural ending to this particular run of whys. They identify my motivation for this project: wanting to help others who wish to express themselves, sharing information I've found useful myself, and updating an area of knowledge that seems to be stuck in the last century. Comparing these with the reasons for wanting to do several other projects made it clear to me that this one should come first, and I went ahead and wrote it, making it available as an e-book on the website www.timetowrite.com. In the process, I also discovered the e-book's USP, the unique selling points that make it appeal to my target audience.

It's useful to keep a notebook for each major project you undertake, with a sequence of questions and answers as the first entry. If you get discouraged during the writing process, it can be very motivating to refer back to these answers and be reminded why you were excited about the project in the first place. It can also help you to avoid losing the focus of the project.

Using whys to create exciting and realistic characters

The same technique can help you create wonderful characters, or, if you are writing about real people, allow you to bring them to life for your readers. You can start with the question "Why write about (name of person or character)?" Then keep going with additional questions based on your previous answers. Here's an example for the central character in my novel *Max Hollywood*:

Q Why write about Max Archer?
A Because he's a fascinating character.
Q Why is he a fascinating character?
A Because he is someone who has had the kind of success and fame most people dream about and he now has to deal with losing it.
Q Why does he now have to deal with losing it?
A Because he's too old for most leading roles, he's gambled away a lot of his money, and his most recent wife is leaving him.

At this point, it can be useful to break this down into several follow-up questions:

Q Why has he gambled away a lot of his money?
A Because he never stopped to think about the fact that someday he wouldn't be a big star any more.
Q Why didn't he stop to think about this?
A Because he's been a total egotist.
Q Why is his most recent wife leaving him?
A Because she was only with him for his money and the hope that he might help her launch her own acting career. Now that he has no more money or power, he's of no use to her.

You can also branch off into logical related questions. In this case, those might be:

Q Why did he marry a woman who was only interested in him for his money and power?

A Because he was into trophy wives — younger women who look great on his arm.

Q Why was he into trophy wives?

A Because deep down he's insecure about being lovable.

If we continued down this line, we could go quite deeply into Max's childhood, his other relationships, and a lot of additional information that could be helpful in fleshing out the character. Naturally, this level of detail wouldn't all appear in your book or script, but it's always good to know as much as possible about your characters.

You can do the same for all of your major characters before you actually start writing, or you can just do it any time you start to feel that you'd like to know a particular character better. I find this a much more organic (and easy) way to define my characters than the traditional approach of writing a full biography for them.

This is also a good troubleshooting tool if people who read your first draft say they find a particular action by one of your characters unbelievable. Ask yourself why the character does what he or she does, and follow up with additional "Why?" questions. Obviously, "Because I need her to do it so the plot will work" is not a good answer! Important actions need to be deeply motivated. If you can come up with good answers to "Why?" questions, it may just be that you need to share more of this information with the readers so they will recognize that your character's behavior makes sense. Naturally, the more casually you can impart this information and the more you can spread it out through your story or script, rather than revealing it all at the moment of the decision or action, the better.

Applying the "Why?" technique to plot construction

The same technique can help you construct your plot quickly. Generally, when you start a new project you have at least a few elements in mind. Typically these might be the beginning, the ending, and perhaps a few key incidents along the way.

If you ask "Why?" about the beginning, you can get a lot of information about the back story—not only the character's history, as we saw above, but all the incidents that have led to this moment. Again, much of it will never actually appear in your book or script, but knowing it helps you construct the rest of the plot.

I indicated that in my novel, the first important incident is that Max Archer's latest trophy wife is leaving him. In my series of "Why?" questions about Max, I filled in quite a bit about him. But if I focus on his wife now, that gives me additional back story information:

Q Why is Max's latest wife leaving him?
A Because he's run out of money and she's realized that he can't really help her career.
Q Why has she realized he can't really help her career?
A Because her support group has told her that she has to face up to the fact that his career is going nowhere. (In daydreaming the answer to this question, the idea that she belongs to a support group came to mind. The group — which I decided to call "Me, First!" — ended up being a part of several elements of the plot.)

I could keep going with this for a few more questions in order to flesh out what's been happening in the marriage and what's led to the separation, but you get the idea.

When you have identified key plot developments, you can work backward from them with the "Why?" approach and quickly generate a lot of additional actions that drive the story. Obviously, there is no one right answer to each "Why?" question. For instance, if you know that one of your important moments is that a police officer accepts a bribe, there can be any number of possible reasons for his action. Maybe he's become bitter about the lack of pay and recognition he gets for his work, or maybe he has a desperately ill wife or lover and needs money for medical treatment, or maybe he has a gambling problem. What you're looking for is an answer that suits the tone of your material and, if possible, one that will surprise your readers yet remains plausible.

When you're brainstorming with the "Why?" technique, you can explore several possible lines of questions and answers. Jot down all of them for further consideration. Only when you've come up with half a dozen or more do you decide which one is the best for your purposes. This will help prevent you from automatically going with your first idea, which often is also the most predictable and least interesting direction.

Another useful question: What could happen next?

"Why?" is the best question to ask when you're working backward from a story point. When you're working forward, the best question is, "What could happen next?"

Let's say you've decided that your policeman accepts a bribe and the reason is that his wife has required extensive medical treatment that has plunged them deep into debt. There's the important action and the reason for it. Now, what could happen next? Again, there are hundreds of possible story paths, but the nature of the story you are telling and what you know about your characters probably narrows the field considerably. Brainstorm at least half a dozen ideas. These might include: the wife dies and the husband decides to reveal his own actions to his superiors; or the person who gave him the bribe now blackmails him; or he realizes that he needs still more money and offers to do more for the person who paid him the bribe. As before, don't feel you need to decide right away which of your options is the best one. Note them all down, consider their pluses and minuses, and only then decide which one to use.

Reaching critical mass

Even if you start with only a few key story points, by using the "Why?" and "What could happen next?" questions, you can quickly generate a large number of plot ideas. Write each of these down on an index card. You can then lay these cards out in the order in which they occurred to you, and play around with them until you have the best order. This also makes it clear very quickly where there are still story gaps that you can fill by asking more questions.

At some point you will reach critical mass—in other words, you will have enough information to feel confident about starting to write. When you know where you are going, the writing process becomes much easier. Many people report that at this stage writing seems almost effortless.

This doesn't mean, of course, that you can't make changes as you write. In fact, it's quite likely that you will. New ideas will occur to you and characters sometimes will surprise you by seeming to want to say or do something you hadn't planned. If these changes are major and you are sure they are an improvement over what you had planned, you can again use the "Why?" and "What could happen next?" questions to develop them and integrate them into the other parts of your project.

Practicing the questions

You can learn a lot by asking these two questions in regard to books you read and films or television shows you watch. When you read or see something that isn't very satisfying, it usually only takes a few "Why?" questions to expose the faulty motivation or plotting that led to the problem. You might want to try brainstorming better answers to these questions. It's shocking sometimes how easily the writer could have solved the problem. To be fair, in films it's often the case that the original script didn't have the same weaknesses; sometimes the director, producer, or star insisted on changes that created problems that weren't there before. At any rate, analyzing failures in this way can help alert you to what not to do.

With successful works, asking these questions uncovers how skillfully the writer constructed the story and may provide you with a useful model for your own projects. Whether you are dealing with a work of genius or a failure, looking at everything this way will help turn you into a pro who doesn't just know what works or doesn't, but also knows... why.

Asking these questions will give you a good start toward coming up with vivid, interesting characters, and intriguing but logical plots. Of course, these are major topics, so the next two chapters will guide you through them in more detail.

KEY POINTS

- Asking the question "Why?" can help you to explore what specific project to work on, to create characters, and to construct your plot.
- Asking "Why?" often functions well for helping you understand the back story and motivations of your characters; asking "What could happen next?" helps you move the story forward.
- Analyzing books, stories, films, and television shows with these two questions will help you understand why good projects work and bad ones don't.

EXERCISE

- If you're not sure which project to start with, use the "Why?" strategy for all of them and let the answers guide you which one should be first.
- Pick your favorite film or book and apply the "Why?" strategy to see what makes it tick.
- Imagine you have been hired to write a sequel to your favorite book or film, and use the "What could happen next?" question to come up with a plot idea.

CHAPTER BONUS

On the website www.yourwritingcoach.com, click on the "Chapter Bonuses" tab, then the "Magic Questions" tab, and type in the code: why. You will be taken to a video of a writing coaching session in which the question "Why?" is used to solve a story problem, and you'll see how to use it as a troubleshooting tool yourself.

6

Creating Powerful People

"How far you go in life depends on your being tender with the young, compassionate with the aged, sympathetic with the striving and tolerant of the weak and strong. Because someday in your life you will have been all of these."
—George Washington Carver

If you ask most people about their favorite book or film, usually they will talk more about the characters than the details of the story. They remember Jack Sparrow long after they've forgotten the plot details of *Pirates of the Caribbean*. They can tell you about Elizabeth Bennet years after they had to read *Pride and Prejudice* in school, even if they don't remember what actually happened in the book. In non-fiction as well, it's the writer's ability to introduce us to memorable people that make an event come alive, especially concerning tragedies like Hurricane Katrina.

Meet a memorable character

To understand how such characters are created, let's see how a classic master of writing, Charles Dickens, constructs a memorable, almost haunting character in just a few paragraphs of description in his novel *Great Expectations*. This is how the narrator, Pip, describes his first meeting with Miss Havisham:

> In an arm-chair, with an elbow resting on the table and her head leaning on that hand, sat the strangest lady I have ever seen, or shall ever see.

She was dressed in rich materials—satins, and lace, and silks—all of white.

Her shoes were white. And she had a long white veil dependent from her hair, and she had bridal flowers in her hair, but her hair was white. Some bright jewels sparkled on her neck and on her hands, and some other jewels lay sparkling on the table. Dresses, less splendid than the dress she wore, and half-packed trunks, were scattered about. She had not quite finished dressing, for she had but one shoe on—the other was on the table near her hand—her veil was but half arranged, her watch and chain were not put on, and some lace for her bosom lay with those trinkets, and with her handkerchief, and gloves, and some flowers, and a prayer-book, all confusedly heaped about the looking-glass.

It was not in the first few moments that I saw all these things, though I saw more of them in the first moments than might be supposed. But, I saw that everything within my view which ought to be white, had been white long ago, and had lost its lustre, and was faded and yellow. I saw that the bride within the bridal dress had withered like the dress, and like the flowers, and had no brightness left but the brightness of her sunken eyes. I saw that the dress had been put upon the rounded figure of a young woman, and that the figure upon which it now hung loose, had shrunk to skin and bone. Once, I had been taken to see some ghastly waxwork at the Fair, representing I know not what impossible personage lying in state. Once, I had been taken to one of our old marsh churches to see a skeleton in the ashes of a rich dress, that had been dug out of a vault under the church pavement. Now, waxwork and skeleton seemed to have dark eyes that moved and looked at me. I should have cried out, if I could.

Some of the language may sound slightly dated to our ears, but the images Dickens created are still fresh. So is his later description of that terrible and memorable object, Miss Havisham's wedding cake. It's a great example of how a setting and the objects in it help to create a character and her place in her world. This is Pip's description of his first visit to the room where Miss Havisham kept her cake:

It was spacious, and I dare say had once been handsome, but every discernible thing in it was covered with dust and mould, and dropping to pieces. The most prominent object was a long table with a tablecloth spread on it, as if a feast had been in preparation when the house and the clocks all stopped together. An epergne or centrepiece of some kind was in the middle of this cloth; it was so heavily overhung with cobwebs that its form was quite undistinguishable; and, as I looked along the yellow expanse out of which I remember its seeming to grow, like a black fungus, I saw speckled-legged spiders with blotchy bodies running home to it, and running out from it, as if some circumstances of the greatest public importance had just transpired in the spider community.

I heard the mice too, rattling behind the panels, as if the same occurrence were important to their interests. But, the blackbeetles took no notice of the agitation, and groped about the hearth in a ponderous elderly way, as if they were short-sighted and hard of hearing, and not on terms with one another.

These crawling things had fascinated my attention and I was watching them from a distance, when Miss Havisham laid a hand upon my shoulder. In her other hand she had a crutch-headed stick on which she leaned, and she looked like the Witch of the place.

"This," said she, pointing to the long table with her stick, "is where I will be laid when I am dead. They shall come and look at me here."

With some vague misgiving that she might get upon the table then and there and die at once, the complete realization of the ghastly waxwork at the Fair, I shrank under her touch.

"What do you think that is?" she asked me, again pointing with her stick; "that, where those cobwebs are?"

"I can't guess what it is, ma'am."

"It's a great cake. A bride-cake. Mine!"

These passages do something very important: They make us want to know more. We're captivated by this grotesque character, and we want to know why she dresses this way, why she has a decaying wedding cake on the table even though horrible insects are running in and out of it. It's the details that add up to a memorable character, almost like the pieces of a jigsaw puzzle. Notice that Dickens allows us to start to get to know this character by using four elements: descriptions of the character, actions of the character, descriptions of the setting, and the reactions of another character. We'll return to these a bit later so you can see how you can employ them in your own writing.

Although quite a bit is revealed about Miss Havisham over the course of *Great Expectations*, I'd be willing to wager that Dickens knew much more about her than he put in the book. The secret of making characters come alive for the reader or viewer is knowing them inside-out yourself. You'll probably never use everything you know, but the more you know, the more you can select what to reveal.

Getting to know a character

The traditional advice to writers has been to write a biography of each of their major characters. In his book *The Art of Dramatic Writing*, Lajos Egri reduced this to a biographical questionnaire that you can answer for each main character. His book was first published in 1946 and its examples are mainly from classical drama, but it's still available and well worth reading. Here is my own version of such a questionnaire, based on Egri's approach.

CHARACTER ANALYSIS

1   Name:

2   Gender:

3   Age:

4   Physical appearance:

5   How does the character feel about his or her appearance?

6   Describe the character's childhood in terms of:

    a   relationship to parents

    b   relationship to siblings (if any)

    c   relationship to other key people from his or her youth

    d   lifestyle while growing up

    e   education

    f   childhood activities (hobbies, interests)

    g   location(s) where he or she grew up.

7   Describe the character's education during and after the teen years, as well as any military service.

8   Describe the character's current relationships with:

    a   parents

    b   siblings

    c   other key people from his or her youth.

9   Describe the character's romantic life (Married? Involved?) and any relevant background (e.g., previous marriages, affairs).

10 Describe the character's sex life and moral beliefs.

11 Does the character have children? If so, describe his or her relationship to them. If not, how does he or she feel about children?

12 What is the character's religious background? Current beliefs?

13 What is the character's occupation?

14 Describe the character's relationship to his or her boss and co-workers.

15 How does the character feel about his or her job?

16 What are the character's current hobbies or non-work activities?

17 Describe the character's philosophy of life.

18 Describe the character's political views.

19 Sum up the main aspects of the character's personality. (Optimist or pessimist? Introvert or extrovert?)

> 20 What is this character proud of?
> 21 What is this character ashamed of?
> 22 What is his or her state of health?
> 23 How intelligent is he or she?
> 24 Summarize the character's relationship to the other major characters in your story.

By answering these questions, you will gain a deep knowledge of a character's past and what he or she is like now. The next set of questions concerns the role your character plays in the story you are choosing to tell.

> 25 What is the character's goal in your story?
> 26 Why does he or she want to achieve this goal?
> 27 Who or what stands in the way of the character? Why?
> 28 What strengths or qualities will help this character achieve the goal?
> 29 What weaknesses will hinder this character from achieving the goal?

Knowing the answers to these five questions will help you structure your story, and we'll get more deeply into that in the next chapter. All the questions up to this point help you decide how the character *acts*. You also want to think about how the character *sounds*. For that, there are three more questions:

> 30 How articulate is the character?
> 31 Does the character have an accent or dialect? If so, describe it.
> 32 Does the character use slang or professional jargon? If so, describe it.

This list can be useful for non-fiction writers as well. If you're writing a biography, for example, if your book answered all of those questions about your subject in an entertaining way, you'd have a very solid piece of work. If you're writing a feature story, you would get the answers to only a few. And if you were doing an in-depth interview, some of these questions would give you a good framework.

Answering these questions is extremely useful, but it's also time-consuming. I used this technique for a long time, and it may still be the best method for many writers, especially newer ones. However, in recent years I've developed another approach for fiction that I find more organic as well as quicker and easier.

Using visualization to find your characters

Using the biography/questionnaire method sometimes feels like you're inventing the character. Visualization is more about *discovering* the character. The word "discovering" suggests that the character already exists, and I think in a way that's true. Consider dreams. You don't think ahead each night and decide who will be in your dreams, what their setting will be, and so forth. They just pop into your head, fully formed. I believe you can use much the same process for finding fictional characters, and my experience in teaching this technique suggests that's true.

One exercise I use is the "hidden picture" technique. I get everybody in a group to decide on a character of theirs to focus on. Then I lead them through a relaxation exercise and ask them to close their eyes and imagine this character's residence. I invite them to picture the front door, and reassure them that nobody is home and they have the character's permission to enter. Then I have them go in and take a look around to see the surroundings. Is the place light or dark? Messy or neat? Modern or old-fashioned? Quiet or noisy? What's the décor like?

Then I tell them they are on a mission. Somewhere in this place there is a picture or photo that is very meaningful to the character. I don't know where they will find it—maybe hung up on the wall for all to see, maybe in a photo album in a drawer, maybe hidden under the mattress, maybe someplace else. But they will be drawn to this picture and they will find it. I stay silent for a moment to give them time to find the picture, then I guide them to looking at it closely. Is it in color or black-and-white? Is it old or new? If there are people in it, who are they and what are they doing? Is there anything written on the back? After a bit more time to examine the picture, I ask them to guess why it is so important to the character. Then I have them replace the picture exactly where it was and leave the residence as they found it. I bring them back gradually to full awareness and have them stretch.

How many people do you think find a picture? Would it be 25 percent? Or 50 percent? Remember, this is not anything they have thought about before. In fact, about 90 percent find a picture, and once in a while someone who didn't find it during the workshop emails me later to say they dreamed about such a picture or had it pop into their mind at a seemingly random time.

To me, this is great proof that your subconscious mind is ready to give you what you ask for. By connecting the left brain, which deals with structure, analysis, and reasoning, with the right brain, which deals with images, feelings, sensations, and emotions, you can come up with characters and stories that are vivid and powerful.

You can go through the same exercise that I do in the workshop. Pick a time and place where you can relax, and just run through the steps I described. It may be useful to have a tape recorder handy and narrate what you see in your imagination as you work through the steps. Some people do find it too distracting to be talking while doing the exercise, but others find that if they don't do this they forget some of the details. Experiment to see what works best for you. If you'd rather have me guide you through such an exercise, for a small fee you can download the "Hidden Picture" visualization MP3 file from my website (it's on the "Visualizations" page at www.yourwritingcoach.com).

The discovery-through-writing technique

Some time ago I interviewed Academy Award-winning screenwriter Alvin Sargent (part of that interview appears at the end of this chapter). I noticed a big stack of script pages on his desk and asked him what they were. He said they were his next screenplay. I wondered whether it was some kind of epic, since there obviously were a lot more than 120 pages there, the standard length for a screenplay. He explained that when he starts a new screenplay, first he puts his characters into a variety of situations that he writes as scenes. These may or may not actually appear in the story, they are more a device for him to get to know the characters and find his way in.

If you want to try this approach, here are some situations you might write about, or just imagine:

- Your character is shopping and notices a teenager steal something. What does she do? Does she tell someone? Does she pretend she didn't see it? Does she advise the youngster to put the item back?
- Your character finds a purse or wallet that has a lot of money in it, but no identification. What does he do?
- Your character is diagnosed with a serious illness. Does she tell anybody about it? Who? Why? What else does she do?
- Your married character is very attracted to a new neighbor. What does he do? If he approaches her, how does he do it?

You can come up with an endless variety of situations yourself and if you already know your story well, you can explore situations that relate to it in some way, even if they're not going to be in the story itself. For instance, if your character is a woman who is afraid of getting into a new relationship because the last one was such a disaster, you could write a scene about the day that relationship finally fell apart. Or if your character is a man planning a huge heist, you could write a scene about the first thing he would do if he got the money.

To base or not to base, that is the question

Some writers base their characters on people they know. The appeal, of course, is that you already have loads of information about these people. You know how they talk, what they look like, how they behave in a variety of circumstances. But there are also two dangers. One is that if your character is corrupt or amoral or disgusting, and you have based him or her so closely on the real person that readers can figure out who it is, you could be sued. The person doesn't have to be famous, either: If they can prove that your portrayal was harmful to them or subjected them to humiliation, you're in big trouble. This is also why it's good to check the phone book and the internet to see whether there is anybody with your character's name living in the city you use as your setting. If you have created a sadistic serial killer dentist named Dr. Frank Ashton who lives in Boston, and there really is a (probably quite nice) dentist with that name living there, he's not going to be happy.

The other drawback to basing a character on someone you know is that you may find it difficult to give them qualities that they don't have but that are required by the story. For instance, your lovely Aunt Agatha may look exactly the way you'd like your character Margaret Finster to look, but Auntie is a sweet and generous type, while in your story Margaret is embezzling money from a fund for widows and orphans. Some writers find it hard to deal with those opposing images.

Probably the best approach, and the one most used by fiction writers, is to create a composite. The character might be bald and portly like cousin Jack, a gambler like your old university roommate, and clumsy with women like a man you used to work with.

If you're writing about characters whose world you don't know, do research rather than just repeating the stereotypes that you see in the movies or in other books. In an interview with Marcel Berlins in *The Times* (London), top crime fiction writer George Pelecanos said:

"The cliché is the cop who is obsessed with his cases, can't have a normal family life, he's divorced, turns to drink and so on. I worked with a lot of cops, the homicide police, before I did this book [The Night Gardener]. *There are all sorts. There are some guys whose lives are falling apart. But there are others who do go home at night and do all these normal things and leave the work behind."*

One strategy is to find out where the people in question go to drink. With many occupations, especially police officers, fire fighters, and people working in finance, there will be a local bar where they congregate. Go there, nurse your vodka and tonic or your Sprite, and eavesdrop like crazy. You'll pick up a lot from what they talk about and how they talk about it. You might even meet someone who will agree to be an informal source of information for you about the more specialized aspects of their occupation.

Revealing character through description

The most obvious way to reveal characters is by describing what they look like: handsome or plain, wrinkled or smooth face, color of hair, height, slim or average or fat, what kind of clothing they wear, and so forth. Beginning writers overuse this technique, and often blurt everything out the first time we meet the character:

Leon was a short man with a perpetual frown on his face. He was given to wearing colorful shirts, often with a floral pattern. His eyes were blue and beady…

And so on, with nothing happening. It's too much description, too soon.

People writing in the first person have an even harder time. Typically they end up with something like this:

> I looked at myself in the mirror as I brushed my teeth. My blond hair was sticking up the way it always does in the mornings, and I thought once more about getting a nose job to fix that funny bump I have. At least my body looked in good shape for my age, 33, and I'm glad that at 6' 3" I'm taller than average…

It's an overused solution and it's clumsy.

When using description, pick out specific, interesting details. Try to stay away from generic descriptions like "handsome" or "attractive" or "motherly" unless you're just giving a quick indication of a minor character. For your major characters, provide specifics. For inspiration, consider the people you know. If you want to make readers aware that one of your male characters is attractive to women, think of a real person who fits that description. What do they find attractive about him? It could be his resemblance to Brad Pitt, but it might also be that he always finds a way to pay every woman he encounters a genuine compliment. When you base your descriptions on reality, you are less likely to fall back on clichés.

You don't need to reveal everything about a character's appearance right away, just the most important or relevant aspects. More details can be added as you go along. However, don't hold back anything that is likely to contradict the mental image your reader has created up to that point. For example, if I describe someone and then only 100 pages into the novel mention that she is hugely obese, that's going to be jarring for my reader.

The remaining ways of revealing character can take up some of the burden of description, and they work particularly well for revealing what a first-person narrator is like.

Revealing character through setting

If you go back to the Dickens excerpt, you'll see that he did describe Miss Havisham, but a lot of the description was actually of her surroundings. The dresses, the general disarray, the rotting wedding cake all helped to give us an idea of the old woman.

If you did the visualization exercise about finding a picture that your character values, you also will have imagined his or her surroundings. You can do the same thing for all the venues in your story. Try to engage all of your senses, for then you will make the scene much more vivid for your readers or viewers, too (we'll go into that much more in Chapter 8).

The same applies to non-fiction. Here is the opening of the article "A Brave Girl Waits for a Miracle Cure," part of a series that won a Pulitzer for Explanatory Journalism for writers Jeff Lyon and Peter Gorner:

> Entering Alison Ashcroft's bedroom, you get the feeling that you are being watched. Stuffed animals are every-where. More then 200 of them fix visitors with a glassy stare from all corners of the room.
>
> Girlish excess? No, good parental psychology. Each button-eyed, felt-tongued rabbit, tiger, and bear repre-sents a time in the last five years that doctors have had to draw Alison's blood.

The setting immediately makes the reader curious and sets the context for telling this girl's touching story.

In first-person narratives, it's normal for the narrator to refer to his or her surroundings as the story goes on. What kind of food he eats, what kind of clothes she wears, what kind of car he drives, whether the apartment is full of light or as dark as a dungeon all help us to imagine the character.

Revealing character through action

I'm sure you're familiar with the exhortation "Show, don't tell!" One of the most effective ways to reveal character is to show us what the person is doing. The situations I describe above, for example figuring out what your characters would do if they witnessed a teenager shoplifting, reveal a great deal about them. If you show me your character at a party, staying by the bar and never making eye contact with anybody, you don't need to tell me in words that he's shy. It will be obvious, and I will feel satisfied that I've figured it out rather than having it told to me.

Let's look at an example from Carl Hiassen, who writes outrageously funny and inventive crime novels. This is the first paragraph of *Native Tongue*:

> On July 16, in the aching torpid heat of the South Florida summer, Terry Whelper stood at the Avis counter at Miami International Airport and rented a bright red Chrysler LeBaron convertible. He had originally signed up for a Dodge Colt, a sensible low-mileage compact, but his wife had told him go on, be sporty for once in your life. So Terry Whelper got the red LeBaron plus the extra collision coverage, in anticipation of Miami drivers. Into the convertible he inserted his family—his wife Gerri, his son Jason, his daughter Jennifer—and bravely set out for the turnpike.

Now, from this I have no idea what Terry looks like, but I have a lot of indicators of his personality. He is conservative, unadventurous, and fearful, and he lets his wife set the agenda. Hiassen never says that: Instead, he conveys it by what Terry does, what his wife does, and the adjectives that describe how they do it. For example, that he "bravely" set out for the turnpike and that he took out the additional insurance suggest how careful he is in life. The fact that he considers the most ordinary convertible in existence, a Chrysler LeBaron, sporty also tells us that he's out of the loop.

Revealing character through other people's eyes

Sometimes it's how other people describe or react to the character in question that tells us about him or her. A worthy example is Hannibal Lecter from Thomas Harris's bestseller *The Silence of the Lambs*. Before the boss of FBI trainee Clarice Starling mentions Lecter, he asks her whether she spooks easily, which of course notifies us that something spooky is coming up. Then he mentions a prisoner, a psychiatrist, Dr. Hannibal Lecter. "Hannibal the Cannibal," Starling says. Pretty good foreshadowing that we're dealing with an extraordinary character, right? The boss then tells her a bit more about how Lecter has outsmarted most of the people who have been to see him, reminds her of some of the gruesome attacks he's committed, and calls him a monster. He gives her the warning, "You don't want any of your personal facts in his head… Do your job, just don't ever forget what he is."

By this point, we can hardly wait to meet the good doctor. But of course, like the expert thriller writer he is, Harris makes us wait. First, Starling has an unpleasant encounter with Chilton, the man who runs the Hospital for the Criminally Insane, and his even more repulsive assistant, an inmate. On the way to see Lecter, Chilton gives her some more warnings and describes a few more horrific crimes he has committed. At this stage we are wondering what kind of jabbering monster we are about to meet, and it has all been done via the reactions of other people.

When we do finally meet Lecter, here's how Harris describes him: "Dr. Hannibal Lector himself reclined on his bunk, perusing the Italian edition of *Vogue*…" A bit later: "She could see that he was small, sleek; in his hands and arms she saw wiry strength like her own." The contrast between what we expected and what we now see is very clever, because it piques our interest even more.

This technique is especially useful in first-person narratives. For example, going back to the man who was looking at himself in the mirror, maybe you would show him interacting with a sister who always teases him in a passive-aggressive way about the bump on his nose. Now we know a little about how he looks and we also know a little about his relationship with his sister.

The character arc

The term "character arc" refers to the change your character undergoes in the course of his or her journey. Especially in films, the protagonist often starts out one way and gradually changes. One example is Charlie Babbit, the selfish man portrayed by Tom Cruise in the film *Rain Man*. At the beginning he cares only about money and resents Raymond, his autistic brother to whom their father has left his fortune. The brothers go on a journey together, and by the end the two men understand and care for each other.

At least in Hollywood movies, the arc generally takes a character from a negative to a positive. Some stories, for example those that focus on how money or power can corrupt, go from positive to negative. There are also stories in which the character's very inability to recognize his or her faults and to change causes a downfall. That's true of ancient Greek tragedies and it's true of *Citizen Kane*.

The change does not have to be a drastic one. Sometimes it's just a by-product of the story. Clarice Starling gains confidence over the course of *The Silence of the Lambs*, but no one would consider that the most important aspect of the story.

Sometimes the character goes on a journey and ends up back where he started, but with a new appreciation, such as Dorothy in *The Wizard of Oz*, or some of the protagonists in the wonderful novels of Anne Tyler.

There are also certain genres in which the character typically does not change. Some action-adventure stories, some spy stories, some detective stories, and some comedies fit into this category. James Bond never changes, even if the actor playing him does. Indiana Jones stayed pretty much the same, except for a bit of bonding with his father. In many television series, the protagonists never alter. In some, characters may learn a lesson or two in one episode, but by next time they have returned to their old selves. Indeed, especially in comedy series, the whole premise of the show may go out the window if the character ever changes.

Despite these exceptions, the idea of a character's transformation seems to be a very appealing element to the reader and viewer, maybe because we've learned ourselves how difficult it is to change.

The character arc is typical of longer formats, such as novels and films. Short stories are more of a snapshot of a moment in time, although it may be a moment when a character comes to understand something new about himself or herself or about the world.

Novelists have an advantage over scriptwriters, because in a novel you can go inside the character's head to reveal what he or she is thinking. You can write, "Suddenly Dan realized that his sister was actually on his side," whereas in a film script it's very hard for an actor to show how he realizes something unless it's expressed in the dialogue. The scriptwriter has to be clever about how the character's actions show what he has come to know. Maybe Dan makes a conciliatory gesture, like sending his sister a dozen roses, or when someone else criticizes her, instead of joining in this time he defends her.

As we discuss in the next chapter, for stories to be engaging they have to give our protagonists a bumpy ride. The same is true of the progression of their change. It has to be interrupted, prone to setbacks, and generally full of difficulties. Even Scrooge in Dickens' *A Christmas Carol* didn't change the first time a ghost showed up. Readers also have to be able to understand what is driving the change. If it seems to come out of nowhere, we will lose our belief in the story.

If you're having trouble with this concept, draw a straight line horizontally on a piece of paper. On the left side, jot down a brief description of the character at the beginning of the story. For example, maybe she's totally self-centered. On the right side of the line, jot down how she is at the end. Maybe she's learned to have authentic relationships with the people around her. Then at points along the line, from left to right, indicate each step of the change and what motivates it. For instance, maybe her mother dies and that stirs up feelings she normally never shows (a step forward).

People who usually stay away from her see her vulnerability and try to comfort her (a step forward). She doesn't know how to deal with this, so she rebuffs them (a step back). Chart the major events and their consequences, both the steps forward and the steps back. Each change should be motivated by something that has happened and that the reader or viewer can witness, although of course you don't want to make what you're doing too obvious.

Nice people and not-nice people

It's not essential for your protagonist to be a nice person; it *is* essential that he or she is an interesting person. One of the things that makes a person interesting is our ability to identify with him or her in some way. Therefore, if you are writing about nasty characters, it's a good idea to let the audience see their redeeming features.

It's no accident that in the opening scenes of the movie *The Godfather*, the Mafia don is shown granting a favor to a poor, humble man who wants justice for his raped daughter. The judicial system is corrupt, so her attackers got away and it falls to the godfather to makes things right. We can identify with and even admire the way he takes the side of the powerless—even if it's not long before he's revealing a less appealing aspect of himself and his family. Of course, the real viewpoint character is Michael, the son who is not in the family business and says he never will be. His slow corruption into becoming even more ruthless than his father is his character arc.

On television, the series *The Sopranos* took much the same approach by revealing the human, vulnerable side of Tony Soprano, which co-exists uneasily with the violence that is also a part of his life.

In *A Christmas Carol*, Scrooge starts off as unsympathetic, but the more we see about his childhood, the more we understand and feel sorry for him, and when his character arc is complete, we are delighted with the transformation.

Alvin Sargent on creating characters

Alvin Sargent is a two-time Academy Award-winning writer whose credits include the adaptations *Julia* and *Ordinary People*, as well as the scripts of *Spiderman 2* and *Spiderman 3*. When I interviewed him he was revealing about how he creates characters.

Q **Do you begin with the emotions of the characters rather than the dynamics of the plot?**

A Well, I think about what this story means to me, how I am affected by it, how I want to project that on paper. Paper is the great enemy. Getting something from your head onto the page is the hardest part. New writers get ideas and can tell you what they want. They can describe some dialogue in a scene that's very good, they have a sense of character, of what the scene is about, of how it moves. But then—and this happens to me, too, sometimes—something will happen between the time that you know what to say and decide on how to put it on paper. The problem is that transition to paper somehow or other has to be eliminated. It has to be, I think, as if it were a Xerox machine so that the image moves directly onto the paper. I guess that's the way I work. I structure later, after I have all this goop from my mind down on paper, just exactly as I feel it, immediate acceptance, not edited and polished in the mind. Don't prepare something before the paper gets it.

Q **What's in this goop?**

A People talking to themselves or with each other, without necessarily any connection to the story. I do a great deal of free-associating. Talk, for pages and pages, I don't know what's going on. Several months go by, suddenly you've got a big pile of stuff as if it were a basket of material, pieces ready for the quilt. I find something alive—I hope. I think too many people are too organized; they've got it all worked out, instead of hearing their characters.

Q **What I've admired so much in your work is the "real-ness" of your people. It sounds as if the process of free-association you've described really puts you in touch with them.**

A Over a period of time, I begin to understand them, to think about them not only in terms of where they are in the story. But I'm sure this is the case with most writers. I think about where these people are today, even when I'm not writing... Sometimes I'll go to bed at night, wonder where they are, how they are, think about the fact that I'll see them tomorrow. Trouble is, sometimes they don't show up for work. [Laughter] You go to the typewriter and you say, "Where are they? What time is it? Why aren't they here?" Sometimes they never come back, so sometimes I fire them.

Q **Do the characters ever surprise you?**

A Oh boy! You write somebody that you can trust, but you don't know them so well that they can't surprise you. It's wonderful! Hopefully, it's more unpredictable than an audience is prepared for... If you don't allow yourself the pleasure of working at it—and that doesn't mean you have to be as disorganized as I am—then you don't give yourself the freedom to find the surprises.

KEY POINTS

- Readers remember vivid characters more than they remember plots.
- You can get to know characters by listing their qualities, skills, and attributes, or you can use the more organic method of visualization, including the hidden picture exercise.
- Basing characters on real people can be useful, but only if you don't libel the real person and you are able to change them as needed.

- You can reveal a character through description, but also via setting, action, and through other people's eyes.
- In many stories, the protagonist undergoes a transformation known as the character arc.
- Characters don't need to be nice, but they do need to be interesting.

EXERCISES

- When starting to create some new characters, try using the Egri method for one and the visualization technique for another. Notice which approach you prefer.
- Pick a character and write one page in which you don't describe him or her at all, except through setting, action, and another person's eyes. Have someone else read this page and describe how they imagine the character looks. How well does their impression match how you imagine the character's appearance?

CHAPTER BONUS

On the website www.yourwritingcoach.com, click on the "Chapter Bonuses" tab, then the "Characters" tab, and type in the code: powerful. You will be taken to a video interview with actor Michael Brandon, co-star of *Dempsey and Makepeace* and star of *Jerry Springer: The Opera*, talking about how actors approach the task of developing a character and what they look for in a script.

7

Story Secrets

"Probably, indeed, the larger part of the labour of an author in composing his work is critical labour—the labour of sifting, combining, constructing, expunging, correcting, testing."
—*T.S. Eliot*

At the most basic level, stories have three parts: a beginning, a middle, and an end. We divide even the story of the human lifespan into young, middle-aged, and old. That division mirrors the typical structure of a story as well, in that we might say youth is the first 20 years, middle age is the next 40, and old age is the next 20 or so. The middle is twice as long as the beginning and the end. In screenwriting, people talk about the three-act structure, and it has exactly those proportions.

Although that division is a sensible and useful starting point, there's a lot more to structure, and in this chapter you'll find out how to hook readers so that they want to enter the world of your story, how to use the Q/A strategy to keep them interested in the middle, and how to give them a satisfying ending.

The premise and the plot

Sometimes people object to the terms "story" and "plot" being used interchangeably. They suggest that the story is what your book is really about, whereas the plot is the sequence of events that you use to tell the story. What they call story, I call theme or premise. It is what you are choosing to explore or demonstrate with your book or script or whatever else you are writing.

In *The Art of Dramatic Writing*, Lajos Egri suggested that the best way to formulate a premise is "something leads to something else." For example, selfishness leads to downfall, or love leads to redemption, or wealth leads to corruption. However, you can state a premise in other ways, such as "love conquers all," or "the child is father to the man," or "your past always catches up with your future."

Reduced to such terms, a premise sounds trite. What saves it from being trite is how you embody it in a fascinating, moving, intriguing, fresh-feeling book or script.

The premise of my novel *Max Hollywood* is "It's never too late to be a hero," but the plot is about an over-the-hill actor who has to decide whether he's willing to stand up for what's right, even if it means giving up his final chance to make a comeback. If a room full of 30 writers each set out to weave a tale that embodies the same premise, I'm sure they would come up with 30 different plots.

The advantage of having a premise in mind from the start is that it acts as kind of a compass. As you develop the plot, you can make sure that the events do indeed embody the premise. The danger of having a premise to start with is that it may incline you to come up with a story that feels preachy or too straightforward to be interesting. If you're not sure what your premise is but you have a plot that excites you, go ahead and start writing. Many authors don't know what they meant to say until they've said it.

If we say the plot is what happens, what drives a plot forward? Let's look at what makes you choose one direction over all the other possible directions at each juncture of your story.

The role of needs

Another common observation about plot is that it's the story of someone who wants or needs something and his or her quest to get it. That's a useful oversimplification that probably applies to the majority of plots. We humans are creatures who want a lot of things. In a 1943 paper, Abraham Maslow proposed a theory of psychology that stated we are all motivated by a hierarchy of needs. In ascending order, they are physiological needs (breathing, water, food, sleeping, eating, etc.); safety (physical safety, but also security that we can provide for ourselves and those we care about); love and belonging (friendship, sexual intimacy, family); status (self-respect, respect from others, recognition); and self-actualization (creativity, morality, spirituality). His notion was that we need to have the lower aspects taken care of before we can move up and concern ourselves with the higher ones. In other words, if you don't have enough food, you're probably not going to worry too much about fulfilling your creativity. Of course, there can be lots of overlap and interaction between these categories. For a writer they are a useful guide to the universal themes that interest readers.

Tales that concern needs lower on the scale will be the most emotionally appealing. That's why so many books and films are about a life and death struggle—it doesn't get any more basic than that. One of the reasons for the success of the film *Titanic* is that it put its characters in a situation where they are fighting for the entire range of needs, taking them from the top of the scale all the way down. The character of Jack is a budding creative artist, so that's the self-actualization element; he's a lower-class boy who wants to be considered good enough to marry an upper-class girl (status); he's trying to win Rose's heart (love); when the ship starts to go down, he tries to save her and himself (security); and when they hit the water it's a struggle for life itself (physiological). As we identify with the characters, emotionally we are led step by step backward to more and more basic struggles. The end of the film takes us back to the level of self-actualization when Rose chooses the purity of love over material things (the jewel she throws into the water).

You can select a premise that relates to any of Maslow's levels and if you tell the tale well, you will find an audience. However, it's no accident that many of the most successful films are action-adventure or horror stories in which characters with whom we can identify are dragged down to the level of having to struggle to fulfill the most primitive and essential needs. Even the most spiritual or intellectual individuals probably still have a great fear somewhere in their brain that they will have to confront these basic needs, and watching how others cope with this is cathartic.

The relationship between need and want

In Chapter 6 I mentioned the character arc, the transition your character makes from one state of being to another. One example is Ebenezer Scrooge in *A Christmas Carol* going from being bitter to being open and generous. This arc mirrors the work's premise or theme. In Scrooge's case, you could say the premise is "bitterness leads to isolation." The intervention of the ghosts wakes Scrooge up to this fact and allows him to change. When he gives up his bitterness and becomes kind and open, he also becomes connected to the people around him.

One of the things that makes a character arc interesting and also gives you an idea for how to structure the plot is the fact that often characters think they need one thing and go in quest of it, only to find that in fact they just *want* it, and actually *need* something totally different. This fits into Maslow's hierarchy, too, because usually what people want is something higher on the scale, but they're not ready for it because they don't yet have something lower on the scale.

Perhaps you remember the superb comedy *Tootsie*, starring Dustin Hoffman. He plays Michael, a man obsessed with finding success as an actor. Early in the film we see how fake he is in his relationships with most women, how he doesn't care at all about children, and his total self-obsession. Most of the people in the business find him so irritating that they will not hire him, so he has the idea of disguising himself as a woman and wins a leading role in a soap opera. Suddenly, Michael has what he wants. But he also falls in love with his co-star, played by Jessica Lange. He can't declare his love for her because she thinks he's a woman, and if he gives up his secret he also gives up his cherished success. The conflict between what he wants and what he needs grows and grows, until finally he is willing to risk giving up his "want" in exchange for what he really needs. And the implication at the end of the film is now that playing a woman has made him more sensitive, generous, and genuine, he may well be more successful as a (male) actor as well.

In looking at the story you want to tell, ask yourself what your protagonist wants. How passionately or desperately does he or she want it? A protagonist who isn't willing to go to extremes (or isn't driven to extremes) probably will not be very interesting. Again, this is one reason so many stories are based on needs on the lower parts of the hierarchy—it's easier to give up wanting to be a painter than it is to give up wanting to breathe.

Is what your protagonist wants in conflict with what he or she needs? At what point in your plot will the conflict between these two elements begin? How can you keep escalating the dilemmas to put your protagonist under more and more pressure? What is the moment of truth when your character must decide which one to go for? If the character never does give up the want, he or she may come to a bad end. Tragedies ancient and modern often are about people who have a weakness they either don't recognize or are not willing to give up.

Who or what is trying to stop your protagonist?

The wants/needs dilemma is a conflict that rages inside your character, although you have to find ways to externalize it.

In many stories, the conflict is between one person and another—at its most elementary, this is the battle between good and evil, as embodied by your characters. Examples include the cop vs. the criminal, the demon vs. the holy man or woman, the little individual vs. the mighty and corrupt corporation. More sophisticated stories deal with conflicts in which right and wrong are less clear-cut. An example would be the police officer who bends the law to put away a murderer, or a battle for custody of a child between two equally well-intentioned parents.

There are also plots that put people in conflict with nature. This is the formula for disaster movies and books, in which the opposition may be a flood, a hurricane, an earthquake, or a fire.

Naturally, you can have more than one type of conflict going on. In the television series *Lost*, the survivors battle the weather, the ocean, animals, the mysterious people already on the island, and each other. And most of them are also struggling with some inner conflict that relates to their lives before the plane crash took place. When you can plausibly involve your characters in several levels of conflict, it enriches the story and makes the reader or audience feel more engaged. However, when you try too hard, as *Lost* sometimes has, you risk losing them altogether.

Who is your protagonist?

Sometimes it's obvious whose story you are telling. Let's say your story is about an adopted man who decides to look for his biological mother. He initiates the action, he moves forward, he encounters obstacles and setbacks, he gets into conflict with someone or something, and at the end of his journey he is a changed man. He fits one of the basic story patterns, that of a person on a quest (a little later we'll look at this story model more closely). Obviously, he's your protagonist.

However, sometimes your protagonist does not initiate the story. Sometimes he doesn't want or need anything at the beginning of the tale, he's perfectly happy as he is. If you leave things that way, it's not going to be very interesting. But let's say that members of a spy network realize that he's going to attend a business conference in Washington D.C. and decide to use him as an unwitting courier to take some documents to their colleagues. Things start to happen to your protagonist that he doesn't understand, and pretty soon he's in deep trouble. Now he has to react. He can try not to get involved, but sooner or later one or more of his basic needs is threatened, and he has to fight. Again, the hierarchy of needs comes in handy, because typically the bad guys will move our man lower and lower on the ladder. Maybe he's arrested (loss of status); then they plant evidence that makes his wife think he's been having an affair (loss of love); then he gets fired (loss of security); and ultimately he gets into a battle for his very survival (potential loss of life). Each step makes him more and more active in the conflict, and by the end, the mild-mannered, perhaps even cowardly man whose only wish was a life without trouble has completed his character arc and found his inner hero.

Once you have decided who your protagonist is, you still have to decide how to tell his story; that is, from what point of view. Let's look at the possibilities.

The first-person connection

One option is to write in the first person. This means that the protagonist relates his or her own story as though writing a diary or telling you about what happened. A sample first-person opening is:

> I looked around. I had no idea where I was. I mean, I knew it was a hospital room, but I had no idea why I was there.

When you read a first-person novel or short story, or even a non-fiction account like a travel book, you feel an immediate connection with the person who is talking to you so directly. That is its major advantage: It's intensely personal. You identify very closely with this person's plight. If he's the man who just wanted a quiet life, let's call him George, and suddenly things start going wrong, you share his confusion, then his anger, and then his determination to fight back.

The disadvantage is that you can only experience what *he* experiences, can only hear and see what *he* hears and sees. In the previous chapter, I've already mentioned how this puts a cramp on getting an idea of what the narrator looks like; as we saw, there are ways around that. But you also can't suddenly cut across town to see what's happening with the man who hit George over the head. You have to come up with all kinds of creative ways for him to get information that he doesn't have first-hand. For example, there could be a passage like this:

> The young black nurse brought me a tray of food that looked like a McDonald's Happy Meal that had been spit out by a toddler. "You had a visitor while you were still unconscious," she said. "He signed in. It was a Mr. Pericles."
>
> The name didn't ring a bell. "What did he look like?"
>
> She stared up at the grimy window. "Tall, shaved head, over six feet. Fifty, maybe fifty-five years old."
>
> She looked at me expectantly, but I still didn't know who he was or why he'd want to visit me. Or how he'd know I was in hospital.

George doesn't know who this Mr. Pericles is, and neither does the reader, but in a later chapter, when he spots a tallish man with a shaved head shopping at the same supermarket, George puts two and two together, and so do we.

The third-person omniscient option

Another option is writing in the third person, in which you describe events like someone who is able to observe everything but is not taking part. In that case, the first snippet might read this way:

George looked around. He had no idea where he was. Well, he did figure out it was a hospital room, but he had no idea why he was there.

Notice that in this example, the person who is telling the story is not only describing what any observer might see and hear, he or she knows what's going on in George's head, too. Because the author is rather god-like, he or she knows what's going on in everybody's head. That could lead to a passage like this:

The young black nurse brought George a tray of food that looked like a McDonald's Happy Meal that had been spit out by a toddler. She thought she'd rather die than eat this crap herself. She remembered the bald guy who'd been in earlier. "You had a visitor," she said. "A Mr. Pericles."

George couldn't remember any Mr. Pericles. He didn't think he knew any Greeks. "What did he look like?"

Martin, the orderly, looked into the room. "I didn't leave a wheelchair in here, did I?" he asked. He hated misplacing things. In fact, he hated working here. Sick people depressed him.

"Nope," the nurse said. "God," she thought, "next time let Martin misplace the defibrillator and get his ass fired so I don't have to deal with him any more."

See how quickly it gets annoying to be in on everybody's thoughts, and how it's harder to tell who the main character is? This is why it's not actually a good idea to get inside everybody's head in every scene.

Third person limited

The alternative, which works much better and is used by most novelists now, is the limited third-person point of view. In this version, you go inside one person's head per scene. You could start as before:

> George looked around. He had no idea where he was. Well, he did figure out it was a hospital room, but he had no idea why he was there.

For the rest of this scene you just stick with describing George's experience. If the nurse and the orderly come in, you can describe what they do and say, but not what they're thinking or feeling.

For the next scene, you can also leave George in hospital and be with Mr. Pericles. It could go something like this:

> Mr. Pericles paced around Room 238 of the Phoenix Hotel, ignoring *Oprah* on the 14-inch TV set in the corner. Mr. Pericles preferred dumpy hotels, they tended to have the most discreet, or drunk, or whacked-out desk clerks. Mr. Pericles didn't like not completing a contract on the first try. It made him feel ashamed.

In this excerpt you have shifted location and viewpoint. If the desk clerk or anybody else showed up, you'd stay with Mr. Pericles' feelings and thoughts only.

For the next scene or chapter, you could go back to the hospital room and George, or you could go to the office of the man who hired Mr. Pericles to kill George, or pretty much any place else you want, as long as you don't confuse the reader.

To sum up: If you're going to write in the third person, a safe rule of thumb is to have only one viewpoint character in every scene. In those scenes in which your protagonist takes part, he or she will be the viewpoint character. If in the next chapter you switch locations and people, choose the viewpoint character in that one. In our example, assuming Mr. Pericles is a main character, all the scenes that contain him but not George would be from his viewpoint.

Just to make sure this is clear, have a look at the following sentences:

First example: The desk clerk put on a fake smile, flashing his yellow teeth. He was thirsty and he hoped Mr. Pericles might leave the five-dollar bill as a tip. Mr. Pericles took it and put it in his pocket.

Second example: The desk clerk put on a fake smile, flashing his yellow teeth. "If you think that's going to get you a tip, you're even crazier than you look, and that would be quite an accomplishment," Mr. Pericles thought, pocketing the five-dollar bill.

In the first example, we are told what the desk clerk is thinking. This would be appropriate only if he is the viewpoint character for this chapter or scene. In the second example, it's Mr. Pericles whose thoughts are revealed, so he's the viewpoint character.

There is another option. Have a look at this:

The desk clerk put on a fake smile, flashing his yellow teeth. It was the kind of smile people who don't get tips put on as a last, desperate measure. Mr. Pericles picked up the five-dollar bill and put it in his pocket.

Who's the viewpoint character? If you assume it's Mr. Pericles thinking the middle sentence, then it's him. But actually it's just the author sneaking in an opinion about the nature of the desk clerk's smile. There is nothing wrong with this, it's a stylistic choice. Some authors do a lot of this and it can be very entertaining; other authors feel the less the reader notices that the author has a personality or viewpoint, the better. But there is nothing to prevent you from mixing some authorial observations in with the ideas and feelings of your viewpoint character if you want.

Of course, you will also have passages that neutrally describe what's going on, where nobody is thinking or feeling anything in particular that the reader is told about. For example, let's say George is discharged from hospital and a taxi takes him home. You might write something like:

> George sat in silence for the entire drive, looking out the window. When the cab pulled up in front of the apartment building, the doorman was helping an elderly lady unload some boxes from another taxi.

Yes, you are describing what's happening to George and what he can see, but you're not passing along his thoughts or feelings at that moment. These kind of neutral sections give the reader a bit of a rest. If we are constantly inside the mind of George (or any viewpoint character), it's like hanging out with a friend who never stops telling us what he or she is feeling. It can become extremely tiresome.

Ignore the second person, please!

I know some of you have noticed that I've discussed the first person and the third person, and are thinking there must be a second-person approach to narrative. There is. In it, "you" the reader are the viewpoint character, and a sentence might read, "You wake up. You look around. You figure out you're in hospital, but you don't know why or where." This is kind of an interesting style for a page. Maybe two pages. After that, it begins to be really annoying. Yes, a few books have been written this way, one or two even sold a lot of copies. Despite that, avoid it at all costs. Trust me on this one.

The role of the subplot

A subplot is a smaller plot that runs parallel to the main plot. Often it runs its own path for most of the book or script and then at a crucial point it intersects with the main plot. It may or may not involve your protagonist, and sometimes it's just used for comic relief or to provide a break from the fast and furious pace of a main plot, or to expand a story that otherwise might seem too small. I'll illustrate this with a personal example.

I am in the process of writing a television film about an avalanche that engulfs a village in the Alps. My protagonist is a doctor who has returned to the village because his life in the big city has fallen apart and he hopes to get together with the woman he left behind years before. Of course, he gets swept up (literally) in the avalanche and the main plot is how he responds and how the crisis brings the couple back together.

I also have several subplots, each with its own protagonist. One concerns the woman's father, who is the rescue coordinator. We follow him as he fails to convince the mayor to evacuate the village before the avalanche takes place, then how he risks his own life to save people, and finally how he is fatally injured. At this point, his story intersects with the love story, because on his deathbed he reveals the secret that had driven the doctor out of the village years before.

Another subplot, this one smaller, concerns the mayor, whose wife is gravely injured in the avalanche. Feeling guilty because his decision not to evacuate the village has cost many lives, he trudges into the wilderness on a doomed mission to go on foot to get help. There is a kind of intersection with the main story, because when we see his body, dead in the snow, at first we think it is our hero who has died (they were wearing similar winter jackets). Then it is revealed that it is in fact the mayor.

Yet another small subplot is about a workaholic divorced businessman who leaves his daughters in the village while he flies out to attend a business meeting. When they are trapped by the avalanche, he moves heaven and earth to get back into the disaster area. For this subplot there is no direct tie-in to the love story, but the theme—remembering what and who are truly important to us—echoes that of the main plot.

It's a convention of disaster movies that they follow the stories of several characters, some of whom do not survive to the end, so this genre is particularly partial to subplots. However, it is not mandatory to have them in every book or script you write. If they help you tell the story, use them; otherwise, don't.

Starting to put it together: The fairy-tale story spine

Some writers just start writing and make up the story as they go along. I don't recommend this, especially for newer writers. If you have used the "Why?" and "What could happen next?" questions, those will have suggested some raw material for your plot. It's helpful to put that into an outline that at least marks out some of the major developments you want your story to have.

Here is a simple story spine, based on the fairy-tale format, that I find useful when I'm first trying to figure out the basic shape of my story. I complete each of these sentences:

1   Once upon a time... *describe the basic setup*
2   Every day... *describe the conditions at the start of the story*
3   But one day... *describe what happens to change the normal course of events—this is called the inciting incident*
4   Because of that... *describe the first conflict that moves the story along*
5   Because of that... *describe what the reaction is to your protagonist's first response*
6   Furthermore... *describe the basic conflicts and escalations that develop, for instance how the events of the story threaten your protagonist, how he or she fights back, and how things get worse and worse*
7   The highest point of conflict starts when... *describe the moment of truth, when things have gotten to the point that whatever your protagonist does now will determine the outcome of the story*

8   Until finally... *describe the resolution*
9   Ever since then... *describe the new status quo—what changed?*
      In a fairy tale, usually the new status quo is that they lived hap-
      pily ever after
10   And the moral is... *describe the theme—this is optional*

The art of the start

When you write the story, you won't start with the first point in
the fairy-tale spine. It is just there to clarify for you what and
who you are writing about. This statement could be, "Once upon
a time there was a mild-mannered accountant who only wanted
to live in peace."

The second point also will not be the opening of your story,
or at least not much of it, but again you need to know what your
protagonist's life is like before you interrupt it with something
dramatic. Going back to George for the last time, if we spend
several pages describing his boring life before the bad guys
decide to use him as an unwitting courier, not many people will
read long enough to get to the good stuff.

It's the third point that usually makes a good start for the
story. A character in trouble is much more interesting than a
character enjoying a routine day. In this case, let's say the inciting
incident, the thing that sets off the story we really want to tell, is
Mr. Pericles putting something in the lining of George's briefcase. George catches him tampering with his briefcase and picks
up the phone to call the police. Mr. Pericles stops him by knock-
ing him over the head with his gun. Someone has heard the com-
motion, so Mr. Pericles has to leave without being able to finish
putting the object into the lining.

This opening scene has action, violence, danger, and makes us
curious about who these people are and what's going on. Or you
could also use the opening I suggested earlier, with George waking up in a hospital, not being able to remember what happened,
and the nurse referring to a mysterious visitor. I find that one

more intriguing, but either would work. George might remember the scuffle later, or Mr. Pericles might describe it to the person who hired him to do the job.

Your opening is vital. It has to hook the reader. If you need to do a lot of scene setting, sometimes it works to have a prologue first, or to have some action that foreshadows what is to come. For example, in my avalanche TV movie, I start with the rescue coordinator flying in a helicopter, setting off some small avalanches in order to try to prevent a larger one from taking place. The power of even a small avalanche is awesome, so this gives us a taste of what we can expect later on, it shows two of my main characters in action, and it provides a great aerial establishing shot of the location where the whole film will take place. Of course, you can do something similar in a novel as well.

If you do open with a routine that the reader or viewer has to understand in order to make sense of the inciting incident, you can still foreshadow that there's trouble in the air. An obvious example might be a happy family enjoying breakfast together, but, unseen by them, someone is watching the house. It might take another 15 or 20 minutes (or pages) before the watcher kidnaps the children, but right from the start we know something is going to happen, and we're waiting for it.

The troublesome middle

A problem shared by many books and films is a flagging pace in the middle. We've all had this experience: We're reading and reading, and suddenly we realize we're just not that interested any more and we check how many pages are left. Hmm, quite a few. And there's another book over there that looks more interesting… Or we're in the cinema, and even though things are happening on screen, we try to make out what time it is and how long before the movie ends. There can be a number of reasons for us losing interest, but the most common one is that the pace of the film or book is wrong. Sometimes it's too slow: Nothing much is happening and we get bored. Sometimes, however, too much of the same thing is happening, and even though it may be full of action, we still get bored. I had that reaction at certain points in Peter Jackson's version of *King Kong*. There was sound and fury on the screen, but my reaction was, "Please, please, no more fighting dinosaurs!"

The solution is something I call the Q/A strategy, with Q/A standing for question/answer. The concept behind it is that when we are reading a book or watching a film, what keeps us moving through it is a series of questions in our mind to which we want the answers. We have a huge capacity for curiosity that kicks in easily, so that when we read even a simple first line, like "It was a sound she'd never heard before," we want to know what the sound is, even though we have no idea who "she" is. The key to effective story telling is getting the pacing of questions and answers right. If by page 5 we still don't know what the sound is, we'll probably lose interest. On the other hand, if the second sentence tells us what the sound is, our curiosity hasn't been engaged long enough for the process to be interesting.

If Q stands for a question that is raised, and A for the matching answer, so Q1 is the first question, A1 is the answer to Q1, and so forth, the pattern that works looks like this:

Let's say the first thing we encounter is a crying infant in a crib. The first question might be, "Why is this child crying?" (Q1)

As the child continues to cry we wonder, "Where is the mother?" (Q2)

We see the baby holding up her hands, wanting to be taken out of the crib. Now we know why she's crying. (A1)

A man steps into the room. We wonder who he is. (Q3)

He says, "It's worse than yesterday." We wonder what is worse. (Q4)

The mother steps up behind the man. Now we know where she is. (A2)

She's not going to the baby. We wonder why. (Q5)

The man takes a syringe out of a medical bag. We know he's probably a doctor. (A3)

We wonder what the syringe is for. (Q6)

Now we see the baby from the front. She has a strange rash on her face. Now we know what's worse than yesterday. (A4)

The mother tries to go to the baby, the doctor forbids that and reminds her of the danger. Now we know why she didn't go to the infant right away. (A5)

If the pattern is Q1 A1, Q2 A2, Q3 A3, then our curiosity never lasts long enough for us to get pulled in. We like to hold two or three questions in our mind at a time, but if we have too many we get confused or overwhelmed. And if Q1 is on page one, and we don't get to A1 for a hundred pages, A1 had better be a hell of an A!

The television series *Lost* has that challenge. In its first season, the writers raised many fascinating new questions but didn't reveal very many answers, which caused some people to give up on the show. Hanging over the writers' heads is the obligation to come up with a really special A at the end of the series. In the meantime, there are hundreds of fan websites on which tens of thousands of people are speculating about what it all means—it's the power of curiosity that drove the series to the top of the ratings.

One way to apply this technique to a first draft is to write in the margin the questions and answers as they come up, and have a look at the pattern. If you're too close to the material, have somebody else read it and note at least their questions in the margin as they arise (later you can add notes on where those questions are answered).

The essentials of the ending

The ideal ending is surprising, yet makes sense based on what has gone before. Masterful mystery writers do this really well, causing us to feel we should have guessed the identity of the murderer, had we only paid attention to the clues that were there all along. Even if you don't write mysteries, that's a good model to use for many kinds of books: Give the reader enough clues to justify how the story ends, but do it so subtly that we didn't see it coming. Of course some genres, like romantic comedies, are formulaic, so we do know the inevitable ending, and your cleverness has to be applied to making the journey enjoyable even though your reader or audience knows the exact destination.

The worst kind of ending is one that depends on coincidence or on outside forces we've never seen before. There's an old writer's rule: You can use coincidence to get your characters into trouble, but not to get them out of it. We will feel cheated if the police just happen to be passing by and rescue the hero, or if, unknown to everybody, at the last minute the bad guy's number one henchman pulls out a badge and reveals he's been working for the FBI all along (I actually read a script with that ending once).

If you have trouble with your ending, the problem probably is with your beginning, or at the very least with your middle. A good ending is the harvest of many seeds planted along the way. If you have trouble with the ending, start working your way backward. For the ending you want to use to make sense, what would have had to happen just before that? And just before that? And just before that, all the way back to the beginning? To see what I mean, rent out *The Usual Suspects* or *The Sixth Sense*. Both of these films had endings that were prepared for every step of the way, yet managed to surprise us.

When the story is over, don't linger. Point 8 in the fairy-tale story spine, the new status quo, can usually be covered very quickly or even just hinted at strongly. In my avalanche script, the reunited lovers kiss briefly and refer to the time soon when they will be together, and then we fade out. Considering that I've just killed off half the village, including the woman's father, it would have been ridiculous to have a long, smoochy scene at the end.

Since your main plot is what everybody is really interested in, you should wrap up the subplots before you complete the main one. Save the biggest and best until last.

Point 9, the moral or theme of the story, should never be articulated in an obvious way, and certainly not at the end. I add it as the final point only because sometimes you may not know your theme when you start, but by the time you have completed the first eight sentences it has become clear. You can jot it on a sticky note and post it where you can see it, so that you never let your story roam too far away from it.

Another useful story structure

The late mythologist Joseph Campbell wrote about a story structure that he found in a lot of myths and fairy tales in the western world. He called it "the hero's journey," and described it in detail in *The Hero with a Thousand Faces*. Script expert Christopher Vogler interpreted it for screenwriters in *The Writer's Journey*. Both books are well worth your time.

Here I will just give you a concise version of the steps in this kind of story. As you'll see, it has some similarities to the fairy-tale story spine, but is more detailed:

1   The hero is introduced in his/her ordinary world.
2   The call to adventure occurs (this is the same as the inciting incident).
3   The hero is reluctant at first—he/she has a fear of the unknown.
4   The hero is encouraged by the Wise Old Man or Woman. But the mentor can only go so far with the hero.
5   The hero passes the first threshold and fully enters the special world of the story.

6   The hero encounters tests and helpers.
7   The hero reaches the innermost cave, a dangerous place. The conflict is escalating with every step.
8   The hero endures the supreme ordeal, touches bottom, may appear to die and be reborn.
9   The hero seizes the sword and takes possession of the treasure he/she was seeking.
10 The road back, the chase—still some problems to overcome.
11 Resurrection—the hero emerges from the special world, transformed.
12 The hero returns with the treasure, boon, or elixir to the ordinary world and shares it.

If you happen to be a *Star Wars* fan, you probably know that George Lucas used this as a template for those films, and you will find it used in many books and films, especially action-adventure stories. It's not limited to those, of course, because the quest could be a spiritual or intellectual one as well.

However, although this is a very useful guide, it's designed to be an inspiration, not a formula with which to fill in the blanks.

The story is the boss

The most important message I want to leave with you about structure is this: Allow the story you want to tell to have its own life and drive and to find its own shape. Everything you do should be in service to the story you want to relate. If you find an already established structure for telling it, that's fine. If not, just follow the story where it wants to go. If you are faithful to it, it will not lead you astray.

KEY POINTS

- The premise is what your story is really about; the plot is the sequence of events that you use to illustrate or prove the premise.
- When our needs are denied by ourselves, by others, or by nature, we fight back, and the more basic the need, the more we fight. This principle supplies a story with the conflict it requires.
- Writing in the first person establishes an emotional connection between the narrator and the reader, but limits the action to what the narrator experiences.
- Writing in the limited third person is less intimate, but gives the writer the freedom to get inside the heads of several characters (with one viewpoint character per scene or chapter).
- A subplot runs parallel to the main plot and can mirror it or serve as a contrast.
- The fairy-tale story spine is an easy way to develop a rough blueprint for the structure of the plot. The hero's journey is a more detailed structure.
- To hook the reader, a story should start with the inciting incident, or at least foreshadow it.
- The Q/A technique keeps the story moving forward.
- The ending should stem from what has gone before. Ideally, it is surprising yet logical.
- The structure should serve your premise and plot, not the other way around.

EXERCISES

- For your three favorite films or novels, identify which of the protagonist's needs were threatened, and in what order. Do you see a pattern?

- In your own life, can you detect any conflict between what you want and what a neutral observer might say you actually need? If so, what kind of plot could come from this conflict?
- Try writing the same scene in the first person and then again in the third-person limited-viewpoint mode. Which do you prefer?
- Go to a bookshop or library and read the opening paragraphs of ten novels you've never read before, and ten non-fiction books. Which openings grab your attention? What do they have in common? Which openings don't? What do they have in common?

CHAPTER BONUS

On the website www.yourwritingcoach.com, click on the "Chapter Bonuses" tab, then the "Structure" tab, and type in the code: structure. You will be taken to a video interview with Robert Cochran, co-creator of the international hit television series *24*, talking about how to use story structure to create suspense and heightened drama.

8

Watch Your Language

"Say all you have to say in the fewest possible words, or your reader will be sure to skip them; and in the plainest possible words or he will certainly misunderstand them."
—*John Ruskin*

After working through the last chapter, you will have the building blocks of your structure. Now it's time to make sure that your words are worthy of your ideas, so in this chapter I'll cover techniques you can use to make your language come alive.

Come to your senses

You may have heard about NLP (neuro-linguistic programming) in the context of business or psychology. It's the study of how we communicate not only with others but with ourselves as well, using our mind/body (neuro) and language (linguistic) in patterns that determine or at least influence our behavior (programming). It was established in the late 1970s by Richard Bandler and John Grinder, and now has many practitioners all over the world.

One of the basic tenets of NLP is that individuals have their own way of encoding their experience, using a combination of their visual, auditory, kinesthetic, gustatory, and olfactory representational systems. In other words, sight, sound, touch (and feelings), taste, and smell. Often people unwittingly reveal which system they depend on the most by the terminology they use. For example, one person might say, "Yes, I see what you mean," another might say, "I hear what you're saying," another might say, "Yeah, I have a good feeling about that," another might say, "That sounds like a sweet deal," while another might say, "I think that idea stinks!"

NLP suggests that one way to establish rapport with a person is to figure out what his or her primary representation system is, and use language that matches that system. Naturally, you can't know which system a reader prefers, so your strategy has to be to make sure that most strategies, if not all, are represented in what you write, preferably quickly so that you hook the reader. You should then continue to appeal to several senses to make the reading experience compelling and involving for all readers.

Let's revisit Charles Dickens and the scene in *Great Expectations* in which the narrator, Pip, is taken to a room in Miss Havisham's house. This time, notice how Dickens appeals to various senses:

> It was spacious, and I dare say had once been handsome, but every discernible thing in it was covered with dust and mould, and dropping to pieces. The most prominent object was a long table with a tablecloth spread on it, as if a feast had been in preparation when the house and the clocks all stopped together. An epergne or centrepiece of some kind was in the middle of this cloth; it was so heavily overhung with cobwebs that its form was quite undistinguishable; and, as I looked along the yellow expanse out of which I remember its seeming to grow, like a black fungus, I saw speckled-legged spiders with blotchy bodies running home to it, and running out from it, as if some circumstances of the greatest public importance had just transpired in the spider community.
>
> I heard the mice too, rattling behind the panels, as if the same occurrence were important to their interests. But, the blackbeetles took no notice of the agitation, and groped about the hearth in a ponderous elderly way, as if

they were short-sighted and hard of hearing, and not on terms with one another.

These crawling things had fascinated my attention and I was watching them from a distance, when Miss Havisham laid a hand upon my shoulder. In her other hand she had a crutch-headed stick on which she leaned, and she looked like the Witch of the place.

"This," said she, pointing to the long table with her stick, "is where I will be laid when I am dead. They shall come and look at me here."

With some vague misgiving that she might get upon the table then and there and die at once, the complete realization of the ghastly waxwork at the Fair, I shrank under her touch.

"What do you think that is?" she asked me, again pointing with her stick; "that, where those cobwebs are?"

"I can't guess what it is, ma'am."

"It's a great cake. A bride-cake. Mine!"

There is a wealth of visual information, there are sounds like the mice behind the paneling, and there is touch, her hand on his shoulder. Although Dickens doesn't mention smells, I found myself imagining a musty odor when he describes the mold, and experienced a revulsion in my sense of taste when I pictured an ancient wedding cake with bugs running in and out of it. It's a fine example of how descriptions from one representational system can evoke responses in other representational systems.

Scriptwriters might object that for them, the kinesthetic, olfactory, and gustatory present a bigger problem. Surely to indicate anything that can't actually be seen is breaking a cardinal rule of scriptwriting? After all, the audience won't be able to touch, smell, or taste what's on the screen. However, the first audience for your script is not film goers, it's the potential buyers of the script. Your mission is to provide them with an exciting reading experience that allows the movie to unfold in their minds.

Let's look at an example from the film world. Here's the opening of one of my favorite films, *Atlantic City*, written by John Guare, as published in the now-defunct *Scenario* magazine:

```
CLOSE-UP: A bright yellow lemon. A woman's
hand takes a knife and slices it into quar-
ters. She flicks on a cassette player. Maria
Callas  sings  "Casta  Diva"  from  Bellini's
"Norma". The camera pulls back to reveal

INT. SALLY'S APARTMENT - NIGHT
SALLY standing in front of a sink by an open
window. She is quite beautiful. She squeezes
the lemon juice into her palms and rubs the
juice on her shoulders and breasts and arms.
She washes herself carefully.

The camera pulls out of the window across the
air shaft into

INT. LOU'S APARTMENT - NIGHT
A man in his 60's stands in his dark room
watching her. He smokes an unfiltered ciga-
rette. His name is LOU.
```

Guare writes like a novelist and does a few things for which the typical screenwriting teacher would slap his hand: indicating camera moves, specifying a particular piece of music, and putting in details like the unfiltered cigarette that the audience probably would not notice. However, doesn't it create a mood and get us wondering who these people are? The visual is there with the strong color of the lemon. Taste may have come into it, too, if you thought about that juicy, sour lemon for a second. You may even have imagined its smell. The opera music provides the sound, and the juxtaposition of the two scenes creates a feeling of unease in the viewer/reader—why is the older man watching Sally? Is he a voyeur, or does he have a more sinister motive? That's all in less than a quarter of a script page.

As a writer, the way you create may also come, initially at least, predominantly through one of the representational systems. The visual is probably the most common. Novelist and screenwriter Joan Didion (*Play It as It Lays*, *Close Up and Personal*) told National Public Radio in the United States that she always starts with a mental image. She writes to find out what's going on in that image. For her book *Run River*, the picture was of a house on a river in hot weather, a woman upstairs, a man downstairs, and they weren't talking to each other. For *Play It as It Lays*, the picture was of a blonde girl in a white, halter-neck dress being paged at 1 o'clock in the morning in a Las Vegas casino. For *A Book of Common Prayer*, it was of the Panama airport at 6 a.m., heat steaming up from the tarmac.

Other writers may find a starting point in something they overhear, or a smell or taste that evokes certain memories (remember Proust?).

Even the kinesthetic can be the starting point. In *Written By*, the journal of the Writers Guild of America, West, Alan Ball recounted an incident that was part of the genesis of the film *American Beauty*:

> "*I met a metaphysical bag outside the World Trade Center. I was by myself and just walking to the subway stop, and this bag just started moving around me, and I thought, well, that's weird. And it literally did it for ten minutes. Depending on how you want to look at it, it was a coincidence. But it was very striking, and it struck me. I was sort of in that moment kind of overwhelmed with this immediate and completely unexpected emotional response because I was a very jaded and cynical New Yorker. I just remember it staying with me and feeling like I was in the presence of something. And even as I say this to you right now, I understand exactly how insane that sounds.*"

To write more powerful books, stories, and scripts, it is useful to pay attention to all your senses and to give an image, sound, or other impulse time to form. These impulses don't come up just when you are sitting down to write. They show up, as Ball's example illustrates, at inconvenient times. It is easy to dismiss them, especially when other people are present, or when you feel you really should be thinking of something else. I find it useful to think about such impulses again in the space between being awake and going to sleep, or vice versa, at times when my mind is fluid.

If you are having trouble writing a scene, try switching to a different representational system. If you can't decide what the characters should be saying to each other, for example, imagine what each person is seeing, hearing, smelling, tasting, and feeling. Do this for each character in the scene, and you may find when you step back into the writer's viewpoint, the scene has fresh energy.

Life is in the details

Appealing to the various senses integrates well with another element that makes writing come alive: vivid, interesting details. Think back to the last time someone told you about their vacation. If they stuck to generalities, such as "We spent a lot of time on the beach, it was very hot and we were pestered a bit by vendors. One was selling religious things," the description just washes over you.

Compare that to someone who says, "The beach was swarming with vendors. One was a short black man who'd bleached his hair blond, and he had a battered suitcase that he flipped open with a flourish like a magician. And do you know what he was selling? Crucifixes carved out of soap!" Now the scene comes alive, you see the vendor, you imagine his movements, and you can picture the objects he's selling.

Many newer writers express themselves with language that's general and bland. Let's face it, most people's lives are general and bland. They wake up, they put on the same kind of clothes they put on yesterday, they have the same breakfast they had yesterday, they take the same route to work they took yesterday, and they show up and do much the same kind of work they did yesterday. They don't want that from their books or stories or films—they want something different, vivid, interesting, exciting. And they want it described in language that is vivid, interesting, and exciting. Here's an admittedly extreme example, from journalist/novelist Tom Wolfe. This excerpt is from "The Peppermint Lounge Revisited." He describes some New Jersey teenagers:

> All right, girls, into your stretch nylon denims! You know the ones—the ones that look like they were designed by some leering, knuckle-rubbing old tailor with a case of workbench back... Next, hoist up those bras, up to the angle of a Nike missile launcher. Then get into the cable-knit mohair sweaters, the ones that fluff out like a cat by a project heating duct. And then unroll the rollers and explode the hair a couple of feet up in the air into bouffants, beehives, and Passaic pompadours.

Scriptwriters are particularly guilty of writing bland descriptions. Big mistake, as Tom Hanks points out:

> *"Reading a script is usually as exciting as reading a boiler-plate legal document, so when you read one that makes you feel as though you're seeing the movie, you know it's something different."*

Look for revealing actions

It's not only in descriptions of the appearance of things that your language makes a story come alive for the reader, it's also in how you describe the details of the characters' actions. Talking about his film *Daddy Nostalgia*, writer and director Bernard Tavernier pointed out:

> "The film is based on little things... on the moments of life
> where people meet each other, where people hurt each other,
> where people on opposite sides suddenly have a moment of
> closeness. Those moments look small, but they can be terri-
> bly important. Like when Daddy says to his young daughter,
> who's bringing him a little poem she wrote, 'Go to bed.' It
> may seem like nothing, but for her it's a terrible rejection; it's
> like murder. The film is full of moments like that, little mur-
> ders which we—not just the characters—always do in our
> lives."

In an article in *Writer's Digest* magazine, poet Diane Ackerman
echoes this and goes even further: "There's almost nothing that
can go wrong in a book that you can't fix with fascinating, rivet-
ing details of one sort or another." She carries a notebook with
her and uses it to record sensory details:

> "I don't put in what happened because I can remember what
> happened... The things I will not be able to remember are
> the sensory details—the color of the light on the water, the
> way the eyelashes flicked, how somebody walked across the
> sand, the sound of a mother seal calling to her young."

Of course, we are not talking about adding detail for its own
sake; it has to reveal something important and ideally it helps
evoke an emotional response on the part of the reader.
Bestselling author James Patterson says:

> "As I work with my manuscript, I write all over it, 'Be there!'
> That means to put myself there, feel it all, see it all. If it's
> working for me I'll feel the emotion. I'll get a little afraid or
> spooked, or feel like I'm in love."

While classic novels from the nineteenth century are worth reading, beware of using them as a model for the amount of detail
they contain. They were written before the advent of film and

television, and people read them partly to get exposure to places they would never see. Now that people have seen just about everything on television and in the movies, they tend to find long descriptive passages boring. Elmore Leonard, bestselling crime writer and master of revealing detail and dialogue, says his book sales took off when he started cutting out the parts that people skim.

Elmore Leonard's ten rules

In *The New York Times*, Leonard shared his ten rules for showing, rather than telling, what's happening in the story. Here is a summary:

1 Never open a book with the weather.
2 Avoid prologues.
3 Never use a verb other than "said" to carry dialogue.
4 Never use an adverb to modify the verb "said."
5 Keep your exclamation marks under control.
6 Never use the words "suddenly" or "all hell broke loose."
7 Use regional dialect or patois sparingly.
8 Avoid detailed descriptions of characters.
9 Don't go into great detail describing places and things.
10 Try to leave out the parts readers tend to skip.

He added:

> "*My most important rule is one that sums up all 10. If it sounds like writing, I rewrite it. Or, if proper usage gets in the way, it may have to go. I can't allow what we learned in English composition to disrupt the sound and rhythm of the narrative.*"

The challenge of exposition

Exposition is prose that gives the reader information about the background of the characters or the situation. The challenge is to introduce it in a way that isn't clumsy and doesn't interrupt the flow of the story. There are plenty of bad ways to deal with exposition, such as dialogue like this: "How long have we known each other now, Jack—21 years, or is it 22?" or "As my brother, Leon, surely you know how important this is to me." When characters are telling each other things they already know, it's a sign the writer didn't know how to handle exposition. There are three strategies that can help you:

1 *Spread it out.* Reveal only as much as you need to in the moment. If you ladle out the back story in dollops as you go along, the readers have the satisfaction of putting it all together, rather than having it served to them in a big lump.
2 *Use characters who have a logical reason for asking questions.* Writers like to have reporters and detectives and police officers as protagonists because these characters all have a license to ask questions. However, you can also use other characters, such as a new neighbor, a curious child, or a meddling gossip, to ask questions that provide information you want the reader to have.
3 *Reveal information in emotional scenes.* The emotional content will obscure the fact that you're also imparting information. For example, let's say two grown sisters are discussing who is going to take care of their ill mother. One of them could calmly say, "Well, as the older sister I have always taken care of mother, including when she was drinking so heavily right after I got married." That feels like we're being force-fed quite a bit of information. Notice the difference if this sister is furious and says something like, "It's always been me—when she was falling down drunk, I cleaned up the vomit! Even on my damn honeymoon, I had

to come back because Mama was 'sick'! Where were you? Where are you now, baby sister? In your own little world, as usual!" We're still getting lots of information, but the emotional sweep of the scene overshadows it.

Talking about talking

The most common problem with dialogue is that all the characters sound the same. It's a symptom of the writer not knowing the characters well enough. If you have gotten to know your characters well, you will start to hear them talking in your head and all you need to do is transcribe what they say.

Dialogue has to seem natural, but it's not identical to how we really talk. If you want to prove this to yourself, tape a conversation and transcribe it. You will find a huge number of gaps, lapses, unfinished sentences, and umms and uhs. When our speech is reduced to paper, most of us sound like idiots, but we are so used to making allowances for conversational idiosyncrasies that we don't even notice it when actually speaking. You don't want that kind of incoherence in your dialogue, but neither do you want people to sound like they are totally articulate.

You also don't want to include all the small talk people make in real life, unless that's part of the point of your story (for instance, maybe you want to show that two characters connect only at the most mundane level of small talk). Dialogue should serve several functions: to reveal something about the character, to move the story forward, and to create the tension or other feeling or emotion that you want the reader to experience.

About those "saids"

Elmore Leonard's rules suggest it's a good idea to restrict yourself to "said" to identify who's speaking. In other words, you'd write, "'I'm not here to be your servant,' she said." Not "she insisted," "she barked," "she averred," "she protested," "she mocked," "she whimpered." Also not "she said meekly," "she said boldly," "she said whimperingly." The words themselves, what we know about the character, and the description of their behavior while talking should be enough to let us know how the words are said. Occasionally it's okay to break this rule, but do it sparingly.

You also don't need to attach "he said" to every line of dialogue. If two people are talking, we assume they take turns. You need only add "she said" or "Ralph said" if you think the reader may have lost track of who's talking. So a passage might go like this:

> "Come over tonight," Ralph said. [You have identified the first person speaking.]
>   "Can't," Katherine said, not looking him in the eyes. [You have identified the other person speaking.]
>   "Why not?"
>   "The kids will be expecting me to make dinner."
>   "Let them order in pizza. Kids love pizza."

As long as the alternating pattern continues, you can leave off the "said." If you interrupt the conversation with an action, you may want to identify the speaker who resumes the conversation, to reorient the reader.

Two strategies for mastering dialogue

The most useful skill for someone who wants to write good dialogue is eavesdropping. By listening carefully to how a variety of people speak, you absorb a lot of useful information. There is also a fantastic website for any writer who wants to get a sense of the voices of real people: www.storycorps.net. It features more than 7,000 recordings of people talking to each other about aspects of their lives. Some items are light or nostalgic, some are so tragic that even short segments bring tears to your eyes. Two that I found especially compelling are a pair of prisoners talking about their situation (one of them died not long after doing this talk), and the woman who had to tell her parents about the death of her sister in a subway accident.

The other strategy for learning to write good dialogue, and for using language well in general, is to read. Immerse yourself in the works of the masters of the genre in which you want to write. Read each book, script, or story once for enjoyment, again to analyze what techniques the writer used, and one more time to catch anything you missed the second time (and there will be some things you didn't notice). Once in a while, read a really bad book in your genre. Learning what not to do is also highly useful, and it gives you a chance to gloat a little that you can do better, rather than just being humbled all the time by the geniuses.

If you are a writer, or want to be, it's highly likely that you are excited by life and find things fascinating that other people find boring simply because they don't look deeply enough. Your job now is to make sure that those qualities that set you apart in life also set your writing apart. When you combine a compelling story with colorful and revealing language, pages stop being pieces of paper and become an entry into another world.

KEY POINTS

- Using language that appeals to all the senses creates rapport with the reader.
- Writing comes alive when you provide specific, colorful details of appearance and action.
- Exposition should be parceled out only as needed, and can be cloaked by an emotional scene.
- If you know your characters well enough, writing their dialogue becomes easy.
- Avoid any dialogue attributions other than "said." When it's clear who is speaking, you can leave off the "said" as well.

EXERCISES

- Reread the first five pages of your favorite books and high-light or note the instances of the author appealing to the senses. How many do you find on the first page? On the first two pages? Have they all been used by page 5?
- Sit in a coffee shop where you can watch the passers-by. For each, select one detail of their appearance or actions that makes them interesting.
- Assume that in writing an exchange between two hostile neighbors you need to reveal the history of their feud. Try writing the scene in a way that makes this exposition as unobtrusive as possible.

CHAPTER BONUS

On the website www.yourwritingcoach.com, click on the "Chapter Bonuses" tab, then the "Language" tab, and type in the code: language. You will be taken to a video interview with NLP practitioner and personal coach Alice Mallorie, discussing advanced NLP techniques for capturing and holding the attention of the reader.

Take Two

> "Creativity is allowing yourself to make mistakes. Art is knowing which ones to keep."
>
> —Scott Adams

No less a master than John Irving has said, "Revision is the soul of editing and, as a novelist, rewriting is three-quarters of my life." Hardly anyone is such a genius that his or her work springs forth fully formed and perfect. Therefore, rewriting is essential, but it can also be daunting. It's natural to fear that what you have written will be fatally flawed, beyond repair. Yet with enough time and skill, you can shape up even the roughest of first drafts. There are reliable techniques for doing this, as you'll see in this chapter.

Do it at the right time

The right time to start thinking about rewriting is when you have finished your first draft. This may sound obvious, but many writers start rewriting while the work is still in progress. It's fine to reread what you've done, and even to jot notes in the margin about how you want to change it in the next draft. But if you start compulsively rewriting the previous bits, you will probably find that your progress slows down drastically or even grinds to a stop.

If at all possible, give yourself some time away from the project before you sit down to rewrite it. Ideally, work on something else during that break, so that when you return to the first project you come back fresh. How long a break it should be is up to you, and of course also depends on whether you have a

deadline for delivering the finished product. I suggest a minimum of a week and a maximum of a couple of months. Any
shorter than that and your mind won't be clear; any longer and
your passion for the project may have waned.

Get into a different state of mind

The mental state required for analysis is different from that
required for creation. The former is objective, the latter is subjec-
tive. The problem is that when we reread what we have done, we
remember what we were thinking and feeling while writing it,
and that automatically puts us back into the creating state. You
want to distance yourself as much as possible from that original
frame of mind. There are several things you can do:

- *Print out the material in a different typeface or on different-
  colored paper.* This is the version you will read and on which
  you will note your reactions. When you move on to doing
  the next draft, use a printout in the original font and color
  of paper, to signal to yourself that you're back in the creative
  mode. Don't try to read your work only on the computer
  screen, a printout is essential.
- *Read the work in a different setting from the one in which you
  wrote it.* This could mean going to a coffee shop or library
  (assuming those are not where you wrote), or just into a different room in your home.
- *Read the material in a different physical position than when
  you wrote it.* If you write while seated at a desk, critique the
  material while sitting back on a sofa or standing up.
- *Give it a quick first rereading without making any notes.* Try
  to simulate the way an eventual reader will experience the
  work. When you've finished this first rereading, jot down
  your overall feeling about it.
- *Then read it again more carefully and make the kind of notes
  you might make when critiquing a friend's work.* For instance,

you might jot a question mark by a sentence you think is not clear, or underline a word you think should be replaced, or note phrases, like "too bland" or "too slow." At this stage don't try to fix anything. This is the critiquing part of the process, not yet the rewriting phase.

⌀ *Reread the material several times, at different times of day.* This could be once when you first wake up, and once again much later in the day. You may find that the variation in your mental state at different times of day yields different reactions to your own work. Reading it out loud at least once will help you check how the dialogue sounds. You might want to read it into a tape recorder and hear it back.

⌀ *For a longer work, it can be helpful to outline it briefly now, even if you wrote it from an outline you made at the start.* Usually in the course of writing you will have made some changes from the original plan, and having a new brief outline can help you get a fresh overview of the project.

Get feedback from others, carefully

Getting an objective person to read your work can be very helpful. Often your mother or your spouse or partner is not the ideal choice. They may give you only positive comments because they love you, or if they give you negative comments it might corrode the relationship. If they can be objective and you can take negative comments from them without resentment, you are lucky because you have an easily accessible source of feedback. Ian Rankin, author of the Inspector Rebus novels, told *The Times* (London):

> "The first person to read my novels is usually my wife; the second or third draft. She reads a lot of crime fiction, so can usually spot glitches and things I've nicked from other writers."

It's useful to have a colleague or two, even internet buddies, who can give you their reactions. These don't have to be writers. If you have written a thriller and have acquaintances who love to read that genre, you've found the perfect audience. Don't ask them what's wrong or how to fix it, just get their reactions to what they read. Did the opening grab them? Was there any point at which they would have stopped reading if it hadn't been written by someone they know? How did they feel about the characters? Which ones did they find most interesting, which least interesting?

The danger that comes with getting comments from other writers is that often they start telling you how they would have written the piece, not how you can improve the way you have written it. If they start suggesting changes, ask them what problem that change is designed to solve. For example, if they say, "I think you should cut Chapter 13," ask them why they feel that would be a good idea. They might say, "It feels like it's not really related to the plot," or "I found the description really boring and long-winded." Even if their solution isn't right, they may be on to a problem that does require attention.

Some writers show drafts to an agent, although not necessarily first drafts. On the other hand, Audrey Niffenegger, author of *The Time Traveler's Wife*, says, "My agent doesn't see anything until I think it's done."

When you get comments, listen and take notes. Write down the positive comments as well as the negative ones. When you get a negative comment, don't defend what you wrote or explain why you wrote it that way. Write down every comment even if you already know that you don't agree with it, otherwise the person who is being generous enough to give you their input will notice that you're censoring it. Also, it may turn out that a comment that sounds irrelevant or incorrect at first turns out to make more sense later.

Organize your notes

When you have gathered feedback from yourself and others, take your pages of notes and organize the comments into categories, such as "characters," "language," "pacing," and "dialogue." This will help you identify which comments came up repeatedly and you'll be able to see which areas require the most additional work. Probably you will also have a big category of miscellaneous comments left over to address separately. If this is a long list, don't worry, you can tackle it step by step.

You may have some conflicting notes. Maybe one person thought the opening was too slow, another thought you jumped into the story too fast. At this stage you will have to use your gut feeling. This is your project, not anybody else's. By all means, use every comment that resonates with you, but remember that *your* name will be on the book, script, story, or article, and *you* have to decide what to change and how to change it.

Start with the big stuff

It makes sense to start with the biggest issues first. If you have realized that there is a large hole in your plot that requires some significant changes in the first six chapters of your novel, for instance, it doesn't make sense to begin tinkering with the dialogue. Similarly, if you've realized that your self-help book isn't organized in a way that best allows readers to build new behaviors into their lives, this isn't the time to make adjustments to your wording. It's a bit like rebuilding a house—you have to make sure that the foundation and the basic structure are sound before you concern yourself with the décor. Structural fixes are easier to make on an outline than on a full manuscript. Rewrite the outline until you have a solid structure, then you can use that new outline to help you rewrite all the sections that require attention. Work your way from the biggest changes down to the smallest ones. However, don't expect this to be a totally neat, linear process. Every time you change one element, you need to consider what implications it has for everything else. For instance, in the novel I'm working on at the moment, originally my protagonist was out of work. When I reread it, it became clear to me that I could reveal more of his personality if he had a job in a fast-food restaurant. That required me to write some new scenes, but it also affected his ability to see his girlfriend at certain times, what he talked about with his friends (since it's natural for us to discuss our work), and it suggested a new character in the form of a workmate. If building a house is a suitable analogy for the first steps of the rewriting process, perhaps assembling a jigsaw puzzle is a better analogy for the later stages.

If you get stuck, move on

The jigsaw puzzle comparison is also apt for another situation that comes up sometimes when rewriting. If you have a piece of a puzzle that just doesn't seem to fit, you put it aside and go back to it later. By then, enough other parts of the puzzle may be in place that you can figure out where that piece fits, too. The same happens in a rewrite sometimes, so don't obsess over one element that doesn't seem to be working. Move on to other parts of the rewrite and go back later. It may also be helpful to reread the sections of this book that deal with whatever aspect of your writing you're addressing at the time.

Be ruthless

One of the biggest complaints publishers have about manuscripts is that they are overwritten. This is fine for a first draft, when you are trying to get down all of your thoughts. However, in the rewrite you need to be ruthless and cut anything that duplicates what's already there or isn't relevant. An editor friend of mine says, "Many non-fiction book manuscripts submitted to us aren't books at all—they're puffed-up articles, and that's why we reject them." If your editing reveals that you don't have enough material for a book, you'll have to expand the topic or dig deeper.

Know when to stop

Let's face it: Your novel or short story or script or any other kind of writing will never be perfect. Be patient, rewrite as often as necessary, but also know that there is a time when it's as good as it's ever going to be. In fact, there is a point beyond which you will start making it worse. There is no rule to follow in order to know when to stop, other than listening to your intuition. Keep a copy of every major draft you do, so that if it turns out you did take your work a step too far, you can go back. If you don't want to have that much paper around, at least save each draft on your computer. To make it easier to keep track of various versions, I put the date into the title when I save a draft.

Needless to say, you should be backing up your files frequently. Periodically, also copy all your important files onto two CDs, one to keep and one to give to a friend to stash somewhere. I learned this the hard way years ago. I made back-up disks of all my important files, and I hid them in a closet upstairs so that if a thief made off with my computer, at least I'd still have everything on disk. I didn't count on the fire that reduced the computer to a lump of melted metal and the disks to ashes.

Move forward to keep from moving backward

Once you start sending out your manuscript or script, move on to writing the next project. This will help you avoid the temptation to go back and make changes to the first project every time it gets rejected. Certainly, it makes sense to go back if you get several rejections that identify the same problem. At that point you may want to make some adjustments before sending it out again. Otherwise, onward and upward!

KEY POINTS

- The time to start rewriting is when you have finished a first draft, not while you're still working on that draft.
- When you critique your draft, get into a different mental and physical state from when you wrote it. This will help you be more objective.
- Get feedback from others, but make all the final decisions yourself.
- Start by addressing the biggest problems first, and work your way down to the smallest ones.
- Cut so that there is no duplication or overwriting. If that leaves you short, expand the topic or dig deeper.
- Know when to stop; at some point, continuing to rewrite becomes counterproductive.

EXERCISE

- Experiment with different ways to change your mental and physical state when critiquing your own material, to find out what works best.
- If you have a hard time getting into the right analytical frame of mind, start by critiquing someone else's book or script, then immediately go on to yours.

CHAPTER BONUS

On the website www.yourwritingcoach.com, click on the "Chapter Bonuses" tab, then the "Rewriting" tab, and type in the code: rewriting. You will be taken to an exclusive video interview with journalist Rupert Widdicombe, who has written for the London *Sunday Times*, the *Guardian*, and many others. He will share the useful techniques he has learned while rewriting under deadline pressure.

PART III
PERSIST!

"The future belongs to those who believe in the beauty of their dreams."

—*Eleanor Roosevelt*

Making a career as a writer is a long-term effort, bigger than any one writing project. It requires a set of skills beyond just a way with words. That's why this section includes a lot of topics that most writing books ignore or skate over. These include how to create a writing space that fosters your creativity, and also how to get your friends and family to be part of your support system (or find others who will play that important role). Another point that many books avoid discussing is rejection. It's a fact of life for writers, but fortunately there are also effective ways to deal with critics—including the inner critic, who often is the harshest one of all. Being a writer also requires you to use your time well. Most time management approaches are not geared to right-brain people, but the system in this book is designed specifically for creative individuals. Finally, being a writer requires endurance, and the chapter on keeping on will equip you with the tools you need to make a success of your writing career over the long term.

10

Find the Write Space

"Be it ever so humble, there's no place like home."
                              —*John Howard Payne*
"Except possibly when you're trying to write."
                              —*Anonymous*

If you have a wonderful office somewhere to retreat to—mahogany paneling, fieldstone fireplace, walls lined with books, a view of the restless sea, an assistant fielding phone calls in the adjoining office—skip this chapter. But the odds are that your writing space is less than ideal. Nonetheless, it's important to find or create an environment that supports your creativity instead of fighting it.

Successful writers vary greatly in terms of the conditions they need in order to get their work done:

- Actress Marilu Henner has written several books about fitness and health. She told an interviewer, "The quiet and calm of a closed-door office? That would drive me crazy!" She scatters her notes and materials all over her house, sometimes storing folders and files in her bathtub.
- Nora Roberts, who has over 145 million copies of her books in print, started writing when her children were three and six years old, and she says her only office was a notebook: "I could be where my kids were, keep them from murdering each other and get some of my story down."
- Novelist Isabel Allende now has a writing room into which she doesn't allow anyone else, but she wrote her best-known novel, *House of Spirits*, in her kitchen. She has also worked in closets, cars, and coffee shops.

✐ Other writers are more particular. Ian Rankin says he can only write at his home office in Edinburgh or his farmhouse in France.

You will have to determine where you fall on this spectrum, but wherever it is, there are ways for you to influence your surroundings to make them more supportive.

Writing at home

Naturally, the ideal situation for working from home is to have a separate study with a door you can close, a window on the outside world, and heating and ventilation that keep you comfortable. Many writers, however, have to make do with a corner of a room, or even a dining or kitchen table.

If you have a cooperative spouse and children, working from home can be ideal. Maybe. More likely, the scenario runs something like this: You gain a solemn promise from all concerned that nobody will disturb the writer for the next hour. You retreat to your bedroom, dining room, or broom closet. You get out your materials and start jotting things down. You're getting into a rhythm, this is great. There's a muffled thud from the living room. Your ears perk up. No, no, your spouse or baby-sitter will take care of it. You resume writing. There's the sound of something breaking. Glass. Oh God, don't let it be the crystal vase. No, probably it's just a drinking glass or something. Now there's the sound of a child crying...

What's the solution? One is that you stay, and everybody else gets out. In this case, you are at home, but you must pretend not to be at home. Let's practice. The doorbell rings. You start to rush out—sit down, you're not at home! What are you going to miss? Probably a neighbor who wants to borrow something or to bore you stiff with stories about the unsuitable men her Sylvia is going out with, or some religious person who wants to give you leaflets.

Now for an even harder test. The phone rings. Surely you are obligated to answer it? No. If you have an answering machine, the caller will leave a message. If not, he or she will ring back. What are you going to miss? Probably a call from your neighbor to see if you're back yet, so she can tell you about the unsuitable men her Sylvia is going out with. We have become such slaves to the telephone that some people cannot manage not to answer it. They assume every call could be an emergency. If you must, listen to the message. Respond only if it truly is an emergency. Admittedly, listening to messages represents an interruption and therefore should be seen as only a halfway measure. Work on freeing yourself from the tyranny of the telephone and you will have much more time to write.

Here are some additional tips for making the best of working from home:

- Look for extra filing and storage space outside the room (or the part of the room) that you're using for an office. Does your kitchen, utility room, bedroom, or even bathroom have wardrobe or closet space that's not being used? Naturally, this is suitable only for supplies or documents you don't need frequently.
- If you can't resist trips to the fridge when you're working, keep your supply of tempting foods strategically low. Most cravings are strong enough to send you to the kitchen but not strong enough to send you to the store.
- Post your working hours on the door of your home office (and put locks on the door). Make it clear to your family that nothing less than a major loss of blood warrants interrupting you during those times. If you are using only part of a room, find a way to separate it, at least during your writing hours. For example, if you're working on the kitchen table, during your writing time the table shouldn't be used as a repository for school books or the shopping.
- Put a chalkboard or whiteboard on the wall, so that when your spouse or kids have a message, they can write it on the

board rather than interrupting you. Don't check this board too often.

- Turn on your radio or television to an unused station, or get a "white noise" machine to block out the sounds of what's going on in other parts of the house. You don't want to know.
- Put your family to work. Your children may well enjoy stuffing and stamping envelopes, cutting out articles you've marked in the newspaper or magazines, and so on. If they don't enjoy it, make them do it anyway, it'll be character building.
- Social calls during working hours can be distracting. Alternative one: Leave your answering machine on, monitor the calls, and take only the business calls. Alternative two (if you can't resist picking up the phone when you hear a friendly voice on the machine): Keep the sound on your answering machine so low that you can't hear who's calling. Check the machine once or twice a day and return the business calls only. Alternative three: Hook up the answering machine in another room and unplug the phone in your office. Alternative four (the only one I've managed, to be honest): Keep social calls short.
- Remember to get out once in a while. Avoid going stir-crazy by taking a walk or a drive, or a swim at the gym.
- If you have to clear your materials away when you're not working, use storage boxes and file folders so you don't have to spend any time finding or reorganizing your papers when you next work on your project. Consider buying a computer desk on wheels that you can roll away when you're not working.

The question of noise

Two recent studies in Germany assessed the impact of noise on stress levels and concentration. One, reported in the journal *Psychological Science*, tested the effects on 200 schoolchildren living near Munich before and after a new international airport went into operation close by. Children living directly under the flight path had increased blood pressure and higher levels of stress hormones. The other study determined that office noises from ringing telephones, printers, and copiers reduced efficiency and concentration by up to 30 percent.

If you work in a noisy environment, consider how you can minimize the noise (e.g., move the copier to another location, turn down the volume on the phone ringer, etc.). If that's not possible, consider shielding yourself from the noise. Special headphones that block noise are available. They work best with a steady source of noise. I use them on long flights and they do reduce the stress that comes from the drone of the engines. The cheaper and more subtle alternative: ear plugs.

Of course, you can also choose to listen to music on your iPod or other MP3 player. Sound expert Dr. Jeffrey Thompson has studied the impact of sound on creativity. He says, "The brain looks different if you're trying to solve a creative problem than if you're trying to solve a math problem." He adds that when you play music, your brainwaves try to entrain (match) the speed of the pulses in the music, which alters your consciousness, putting you into a more dream-like state. This level is more conducive to creativity.

The next time you have a task that is creative rather than analytical, experiment with having different types of music on in the background. Try brainstorming for five or ten minutes with each type of music, and jot down your ideas as well as what type of music was playing. Which prompted the most ideas and the best ideas? Repeat this experiment a few times, varying the order of the music, because the quantity and quality of the ideas may also be linked to other factors. When you find the soundtrack that seems to work best, use it regularly for the brainstorming phases of your writing.

In an interview with *The Wall Street Journal*, Boris Akunin, Russian author of a successful series of mystery novels, says before he begins writing he plays recorded music: "I have to put on the right sort of music, to listen to it for five or ten minutes just to get tuned to the right mood." For a tragic mood, he likes Mahler; for a tender mood, it's early Beatles albums.

There's another way to use music. Wait until you naturally get into a good writing mood, then put on a song or an album you don't normally play but that supports the mood. Do this two or three times, always using the same music. Thereafter, when you don't feel in a great writing mood but want to, put on that music and it should create the mood by association. In neuro-linguistic programming, this is called an anchor. Of course, before there was NLP, Pavlov did something similar with dogs and food.

For those times when you want to have music, I recommend www.pandora.com. It's a website that creates a virtual radio station for you, playing music only by the artists you specify and ones whose music is similar. You can also teach it to be better at judging what to play for you by responding to individual selections. Furthermore, you can set up a whole bunch of stations—maybe one for jazz, one for rock, one for country, and so on. Classical music is missing, unfortunately. At least at this writing, the service is free. A similar program that does include classical music is www.last.fm.

What are you looking at?

Several studies have shown that hospital patients need less pain medication and take less time to recover when they have a view of nature from their windows. Even a mural of nature lowered dental patients' blood pressure, compared to just looking at a plain wall. What are you looking at when you're in your writing environment?

Obviously, we don't all have natural vistas to look on from our windows, but it's easy enough to buy some great calendars with scenic views, and to keep changing them often enough that the sight refreshes you anew. If you're not into nature, calendars featuring your favorite animal or pictures of babies may work just as well.

Bringing a bit of nature indoors can also be calming, according to a study done by psychology researcher Helen Russell at the University of Surrey. She gave two groups of volunteers a tough math test. One group took the test in a room with normal office furniture. The other group took the test in a room that contained 27 tropical plants. The group with the plants scored lower on a skin-conductivity stress test.

Even if, like me, you have a red thumb (is that the opposite of a green thumb?), it's a good idea to have a plant or two in your work area. As well as reducing stress, they add oxygen and humidity to the air, and NASA research suggests that common houseplants can convert chemical air pollutants into harmless substances. Recommended plants include ivy, potted chrysanthemums, peace lilies, and philodendrons.

Working away from home

For some writers, working at home is not an option. Fortunately, there are alternatives:

- *Coffee shops*. For once, we can be happy that there seems to be a Starbucks or Caffè Nero sprouting up on every corner. If you avoid the busiest hours, these can be calm environments in which to write without feeling pressured to leave the minute you've finished your cappuccino. Cafés in museums, galleries, or colleges are also good during off-peak times. In many cases you'll even find a power point so you can plug in your laptop rather than depending on its battery. Some writers take an extension lead with them to make this easier. Cheeky? Sure, but why not?
- *Libraries*. Although some of these are facing budget cuts, many are being turned into media centers with computer access, so they are good for doing online research as well as writing.

- *A friend's home.* If you have friends who are away at work all day, you may want to ask whether you can use their home for writing sessions while they are out.
- *A park.* Obviously this depends on the weather, and the light conditions aren't ideal for working on a laptop, but a park bench can be a great place to brainstorm or to edit your manuscript with a red pencil.
- *Your car.* If no other place is available, you can just drive somewhere, park, and work.
- *Anywhere, any time.* If you carry a notebook and maybe a digital recorder, you can jot down or dictate ideas or bits of dialogue whenever you have a spare moment. This turns those minutes spent waiting at the bank or the post office into productive chunks of time. If you have an answering machine, you can even call yourself and leave your ideas as messages to be harvested when you get home. This will be totally unobtrusive, since these days everybody is on their mobile phone 90 percent of the time anyway.

If you regularly write away from home, create a portable office you can take with you. This can be in the form of an accordion file or a briefcase or a gym bag. It should contain all of the documents you need, plus supplies like extra pens, paper clips, a small stapler, and ear plugs.

Ultimately, the only answer to the question "Where is the best place to write?" is "Wherever you can." Try out a variety of locations to find out whether you thrive on a bit of noise and bustle, or prefer to have calm and silence. With a bit of creativity, you can find—or create—your ideal writing space.

KEY POINTS

- There is no one best environment in which to write.
- If you work at home and have a family, set rules about not being interrupted and about others respecting your work-place—and enforce them.
- Respect your own writing time by not giving in to interruptions.
- If music helps you to think or write, use it as an anchor for creativity.
- Have some plants in your writing area to freshen the air and improve your mood.
- If you have to work away from home, try a variety of venues.

EXERCISES

- Don't assume that the place you do your writing at the moment is the best; try a variety of settings and compare how you feel and how well you write before settling on a permanent venue.
- If you work at home, post some writing-time rules where your family or roommates can see them.

CHAPTER BONUS

On the website www.yourwritingcoach.com, click on the "Chapter Bonuses" tab, then the "Write Sites" tab, and type in the code: site. You will be taken to a video tour in which three writers give you a look at their very diverse writing spaces, and tips on how best to take advantage of the space you have.

11

With a Little Help from Your Friends

"People who study resilience in children have found that all a child needs is one adult who believes in the child, who conveys a sense of encouragement and faith, for the child to prevail. And I think that is probably true for artists as well… I think that at some point you do need to be encouraged—told that it is OK to be creating and that what you are creating is worthwhile."

—Diane Ackerman

Usually, writing is a solitary endeavor, but it becomes even more so if the people around you don't understand and don't support your creative activities. It's not rare for aspiring writers to be treated with anything from condescension ("It's nice that you have a little hobby") to outright negativity ("What makes you think anybody would want to read anything you have written?").

There are lots of possible reasons for these attitudes. Some people may be jealous, some may not understand how you can get excited about something that doesn't excite them, and some may be trying to help you avoid the pain of rejection by suggesting you give up before others judge your work. Training expert Dr. Julian Feinstein has pointed out that the world can be divided into positive people (who expect to win) and negative people (who expect to be right). Because most new ventures fail, the easiest way to be right is to be negative.

Whatever the reasons behind them, negative comments hurt writers and sometimes drain their energies so much that they do give up. Let's face it, writing is hard enough without that kind of negativity added to the mix.

My goal is not only to help you eliminate the negative attitudes of other people, but also to make sure you have one or more who are actively cheering you on. Having even one person who believes in your dream can make a huge difference. One of the more eloquent statements about this came from author Thomas Wolfe (the one who wrote *Look Homeward, Angel* and *You Can't Go Home Again*, not contemporary novelist Tom Wolfe). Referring to a time when he doubted his ability as a writer, Wolfe wrote:

> "During this time, I was sustained by one piece of inestimable good fortune. I had for a friend a man of immense and patient wisdom and a gentle but unyielding fortitude... I did not give in because he did not let me give in... At this time there was little that this man could do except observe, and in one way or another keep me at my task, and in many quiet and wonderful ways he succeeded in doing this."

You may not have such a magnificent champion in your life right now, but fortunately there are things you can do to make it more likely that you will find support and encouragement from friends and family. Here are the steps you can take.

Consider the intention

As I said above, there are many possible reasons for the negative remarks people make. Often there is a positive intention behind them. Begin by reviewing the comments the unsupportive people in your life make and try to figure out what positive intention might be prompting them. The most common one is that they are trying to shield you from disappointment, on the basis that if you don't try, you can't fail. Of course, the downside of this is that if you don't try, you can't succeed, either. Many people let fear stop them from going for their dreams, but that doesn't mean you have to buy into their outlook.

Make time for a talk

Find a time when you and the other person are not stressed or in a hurry. By asking them to invest the time to have a talk about their comments, you'll be signaling how seriously you view the issue and how seriously you expect them to take it.

Acknowledge their positive intention

If you feel they have a positive intention, begin by acknowledging that. For example, you might say, "I know that you worry if my writing is rejected I'll be hurt, and I appreciate that. I think that's why you sometimes make comments that sound negative." Or the statement might be something along the lines of, "I know you like to kid around about lots of things, and that's why you make jokes about my writing."

Let them know how their behavior affects you

If you haven't detected any positive intentions, just go directly to this step, telling the other person how their comments or other lack of support affects you. Tie your feeling to the action rather than the person. In other words, instead of saying, "You make me feel like you're not taking me seriously," say, "Your jokes about my writing make me feel like you're not taking me seriously." Behavior can be changed, so focus on their behavior.

They may say that's not what they intend, or that you should have a better sense of humor, or not to be so sensitive. Don't let them sidetrack you into a debate as to whether or not you are entitled to your feelings. You can tell them that may be so, but this is how you feel, and since you believe they don't intend to undermine or humiliate or belittle you, you'd like them to change their behavior.

Be specific about what you'd like them to do differently

It's very important to be specific about what you want the other person to do. Asking them to change their attitude is too abstract. It's much easier for them if you are exact about the behavior you'd like to see. This might be no longer teasing you about your writing, or not interrupting you when you're writing unless it's an emergency, or not referring to your writing in front of friends as your "little hobby." Again, beware of getting sucked into a discussion of why these things aren't really meant to hurt you; restate the fact that they do, and ask that the other person agree to change that behavior.

If you're not sure what you want them to do, daydream for a few minutes about what you would see and hear if the problem were solved. If the people in your life were fully supportive, what would they do differently? Jot down everything that occurs to you, then pick out the most important behaviors and make those the focus of your discussion.

Look for win-win situations

Sometimes this kind of discussion brings out that you need to change your behavior as well. For instance, if your spouse or partner feels that you are no longer spending enough time together because you are working on your writing so much, you may need to negotiate a little. You might suggest that the two of you go out for dinner or a movie one night a week. Agree to honor your commitment to that time and ask your spouse to honor your commitment to your writing time. You might also volunteer to make it easier for the other person to enjoy an activity they want to do; for example, if you have children you could agree to be with them one evening a week when your partner goes bowling or playing poker or swimming at the health club, and your partner can be with them one night a week when you go to the library or a coffee shop to do your writing.

Another change you can make is to take breaks between major writing projects. Use these to catch up with all the things and people you may have neglected while writing. This is the time to send letters or emails to friends, or invite them out for a lunch or dinner (maybe a dinner party if you want to catch up with several at one time), and any gardening or household tasks that have fallen by the wayside. It's also a good time to catch up on your reading, exercising, or other pleasures you've denied yourself. Not only will it restore balance to your life, it will replenish your brain and soul and give you a fresher perspective when you sit down again to write.

Point out infractions immediately

If you have agreement that the other person is going to change, be prepared for the fact that old habits die hard. If the other person slips back into old patterns, point it out calmly and gently. There's a saying in the personal development field that we train people how to treat us. In some cases we have allowed them to mistreat us, but that can always be changed.

To many people, writing is sort of a make-believe, artsy thing to do. Surely it's not as important as helping them to move, or serving on the refreshment committee of the church social group, or joining them for a beer while watching football on television. When you encounter this attitude, stand fast! If someone dares to suggest that you give up your writing time to help them move, since you're "only writing," tell them you'd prefer to help them between midnight and four a.m. "But I'll be sleeping then!" they'll say in astonishment. "Only sleeping?" you can reply. When people see that you respect your writing time, they will respect it as well.

Dealing with children

The six steps above can be adapted to work with your children, too. Make it clear to them that not only is writing important to you, but it's a kind of job (even if you're not getting paid for it yet).

If you're asking your children to give you some uninterrupted time, let them know exactly how long the writing session will be, so they can look forward to spending time with you afterward. A suggestion from writer and mother of three Susan Barnson-Hayward: If your children are young, set a timer to go off in 30 minutes, and tell the kids that when the bell rings you'll stop writing and give them your full attention.

You can also involve your children in some aspects of your work. Older children can help with research in books or on the internet, making photocopies, addressing envelopes, and even brainstorming ideas. Younger children can lick stamps, organize your pens, and sort paper clips. If you get them involved they will understand what you do and feel proud of helping you.

Find like-minded people

It's reasonable to expect your friends and family to treat your writing with respect simply because it matters to you. It's not reasonable to expect that they will necessarily find it interesting or understand your writing challenges.

Who is most likely to appreciate your efforts as a writer? Another writer. If you live in a city, you should be able to find one or more writers' groups that has regular meetings. These can be very useful, but in my experience they can also be a waste of time. Too often they seem to attract some bitter people who spend a lot of time complaining that they can't get an agent, or that publishers don't appreciate their work, or that their writing is too good for the sordid world of commercial publishing. Writing groups sometimes also attract people who love meetings and want to devise all kinds of rules and regulations, so pretty soon you're spending valuable time debating how many minutes each person should have for reading their work, and whether this should be done in the alphabetical order of first names or last names. If you find yourself in that kind of group, flee! Don't kid yourself that you can change the group—find another one, or even start your own.

Find a Writing buddy

If you find someone else who shares your interest in writing, it can be very productive and heartening to form a two-person support group. You can exchange your work and get constructive feedback, support each other in meeting your writing goals, help each other over the lows, and celebrate the highs.

It makes most sense to look for someone who is at roughly the same stage of experience and success as you are, or just a bit ahead of you. If you're writing part-time, a full-time writer may not be a great match because he or she will have different challenges. It's also good to select someone who has an interest in the same type of writing as you, for instance articles, short stories, film scripts, or novels. Each of these has a different set of problems and solutions.

Although your arrangement doesn't need to be overly formal, it is helpful to set up some kind of schedule for meetings, and to limit the amount of time you spend on small talk when you do meet.

Use the power of the internet

Now that almost everyone has access to the internet, it's not necessary that the members of your writing group or your writing buddy live in the same town. There are lots of excellent writing-related sites that have virtual writing groups, forums on which you can share problems and solutions, and ways to communicate with individuals who have the same interests. You can also listen to writing-related podcasts while you're exercising or driving or doing housework. Some of these can be found at the iTunes website.

Attend a writing class

Local educational establishments offer a variety of writing classes in which you can improve your mastery of the craft and meet other writers. There are also many online courses that post lessons and have tutors who will give you feedback on assignments.

Attend writers' conferences

Attending a writers' conference is a great way to meet like-minded people and get over feelings of isolation. Spending a day or a weekend in the midst of people who all share your passion for writing is a fantastic tonic. These events generally offer you a chance to chat with editors and agents as well. In some cases, you can pitch your ideas to them in brief meetings. Many deals have been made in this kind of setting, so you should consider it an investment in your writing career rather than a luxury. You may be required to educate your spouse or partner on this aspect of the excursion, however.

Consider hiring a writing coach or consultant

If you can't find help or support from your peer group, whether locally or online, you may want to consider hiring a writing coach, consultant, or editor. These are professionals who can help you with every phase of your writing project. It's no more strange to hire a writing coach than it is to hire a nutritionist to help you figure out a healthy diet or a fitness coach to help you get into shape.

A reputable writing coach or editor will be very clear about the fees involved and will not obligate you to any long-term contract. You should always have an initial session in which you explain what you want to achieve and what you expect from them, and they let you know what they can do for you and how they will do it. It makes sense to work with coaches who have experience in the field that interests you, so if you want to write screenplays, it's fair to expect that the person helping you will have written some screenplays and had at least a measure of success.

The other thing to watch out for—and avoid—is a coach who tries to steer you in the direction of how *they* would write the project in question, rather than helping you to write it the way *you* want to write it. When I coach writers, I always try to serve their vision of the project, not to impose my own, and every good coach will do the same.

You can have support even when you're alone

Last, but not least, you can get support and inspiration from reading magazines and books on the art and craft of writing and the biographies or memoirs of writers and artists. Many a struggling creative person has gained inspiration by reading the letters of Vincent Van Gogh to his brother, for example.

I hope that you will always feel that this book is here to support your efforts as well. The associated website has up-to-date information on upcoming writing conferences and a list of writing consultants.

KEY POINTS

- We train people how to treat us. If people are not respecting you as a writer, you have to train them to treat you differently.
- You can involve your children in your research and writing.
- You can find like-minded people in writers' groups or on the internet, and at writing conferences and workshops.
- Teaming up with a writing buddy is great for mutual support.
- Sometimes it is useful to hire a writing consultant or coach to help you. If you do this, you must be clear about what you expect, and the coach must be clear about what he or she can deliver and the fees involved.

EXERCISES

- Review your circle of friends and your family and identify anyone who you feel is unsupportive.
- Before you discuss the situation with them, jot down the outcomes you want and have these notes handy. They will help you stay calm and focused.
- If you need more support, make up a plan for how you can get it: a writing class, an internet connection, a writing group, or another approach.

CHAPTER BONUS

On the website www.yourwritingcoach.com, click on the "Chapter Bonuses" tab, then the "Support" tab, and type in the code: support. You will be taken to an interview with psychology expert Philip Harland, who offers additional insights into how you can get support for your writing.

12

Tame the Wild Inner (and Outer) Critic

"I don't know the key to success, but the key to failure is to try to please everyone."

—Bill Cosby

The hardest part of being a writer is dealing with rejection. In fact, it's probably the hardest part of life in general. If you doubt that people are extremely sensitive in this regard, you may be surprised by the results of a fascinating experiment conducted by Lisa Zadro at the University of New South Wales, Australia. The researchers had people play a game of "catch" on a computer with several other people who were also hooked up to the system elsewhere. In fact, the game was fixed: The only human playing was the test subject, and the computer was programmed to pass him or her the ball only twice in an entire six-minute game.

When they thought other players were freezing them out, the test subjects reported lower self-esteem, less sense of belonging, and a reduced sense of meaningful existence. Pretty extreme reactions for a little game, but it gets stranger: Even when they knew they were playing only a pre-programmed computer, they still reported negative psychological effects!

There's no way around it—even the most successful writers had their work rejected repeatedly at some point. Generally, this happens the most at the beginning of a career, but there have also been many writers who had initial success and then at some point found that the demand for their work had dried up. Some regained their previous level of success, many never did. So yes, it's hard. But in this chapter I'll share with you some strategies for coping with rejection so that it doesn't stop you from moving forward.

In addition to the outer critics you'll encounter, such as agents, editors, and publishers, you may have a critic who is harsher than any of them: your inner critic. This is my term for that little voice in your head, or that tight feeling in your throat or stomach, that seems intent on convincing you that what you're writing can't possibly succeed and maybe even that you're a fraud who will be found out any minute. In the latter half of this chapter, I will present a technique you can use for transforming that harsh inner critic into a constructive inner guide.

There are a million reasons...

When your manuscript comes back, or an editor doesn't choose to commission the article you've proposed, often you receive no indication why. Our natural inclination is to assume that the person who rejected us thought the idea or the writing was bad. In fact, there are all kinds of reasons for projects being rejected that have nothing to do with the quality of the work. Here are a few:

- It may be too similar to something they are doing already. If a publishing house has recently acquired a vampire novel, it's unlikely they will accept your vampire novel even if it's good. Even at an agency, if the agent already handles three thriller writers, she may not feel like adding another one. If an editor has already assigned someone to report on the latest trend in teenage fashions, your proposal for a story on the same topic will be rejected immediately. This happens so often that some writers assume their ideas are being stolen. There is the occasional theft, but it doesn't happen nearly as often as newer writers suspect. Some ideas just seem to be in the air at certain times.

✐ It may be that the company is having financial problems and is not in a position to acquire new material at the moment. This isn't something its staff would be eager to divulge, of course. Or they may be about to be taken over, and they don't want to commit to anything until the new regime is in place.

✐ It may be that what you've sent them simply isn't a good match with what they find interesting. There are certain agents, for example, who don't handle science fiction because they don't feel any affinity for it. I recently had a comic novel rejected by an agent who said she thought it was probably good, but "I don't really relate to comedies." The same kind of thing happens with publishers and editors and television and film executives. While it's important to try to find out the tastes of the person to whom you're submitting material, frequently that's not possible.

The moral is: When your work is rejected without any reason being given, don't jump to the conclusion that the people to whom you submitted it thought it was no good. There are a million other possible reasons that have nothing to do with you or the quality of your material.

If you find your spirits sinking in these situations, you can use a technique drawn from therapy. When psychologist Michael Yapko works with depressed people, he has them come up with six possible explanations for an upsetting event. When they realize that the reason behind the event isn't necessarily personal, they often experience a lifting of their mood.

Everybody's a critic

Now let's turn to those times when there is a reason given, and the reason is that they don't think what you've written or what you're proposing is any good. Here's the key thing to remember: A rejection is just somebody's opinion. They may be right, they may be wrong. Even if it's the chief editor of a big publishing house, or a well-known agent, or an experienced writing teacher, it's only their opinion. They've been wrong before, and it may be that they're wrong again. This is proved by the examples I gave in Chapter 1 of authors whose work was rejected time and time again, but who persevered and eventually experienced tremendous success with the very project that others hated. You don't need to make everybody fall in love with what you've written. You need to find only one agent, one publisher, one network or studio executive who recognizes your brilliance. As they say in the dating game, sometimes you have to kiss a lot of frogs before you find a prince (or princess).

When the rejections are getting you down

If that manuscript has come back one too many times, maybe with a snippy note from some 12-year-old junior editor, read the following opinions of books that went on to become huge successes. Maybe in the next edition of this book, I can include some rejections you received and a report of the success you went on to have!

"It is impossible to sell animal stories in the USA."
To George Orwell, for *Animal Farm*

"The book is much too long. There are too many long speeches... I regret to say that the book is unsaleable and unpublishable."
To Ayn Rand, for *Atlas Shrugged*

"We are not interested in science fiction which deals with negative utopias. They do not sell."
To Stephen King, for *Carrie*

"I haven't really the foggiest idea about what the man is trying to say... Apparently the author intends it to be funny—possibly even satire—but it is really not funny on any intellectual level... From your long publishing experience you will know that it is less disastrous to turn down a work of genius than to turn down talented mediocrities."
Regarding Joseph Heller, *Catch-22*

"Too different from the other [books for] juveniles on the market to warrant its selling."
To Dr. Seuss for *And to Think I Saw It on Mulberry Street*

"It does not seem to us that you have been wholly successful in working out an admittedly promising idea."
To William Golding for *Lord of the Flies*

"The girl doesn't, it seems to me, have a special perception or feeling which would lift that book above the 'curiosity' level."
Regarding *The Diary of Anne Frank*

"I'm sorry, Mr. Kipling, but you just don't know how to use the English language."
To Rudyard Kipling for *The Jungle Book*

"We have read the chapters of Mr. Joyce's novel with great interest, and we wish we could offer to print it. But the length is an insuperable difficulty to us at present. We can get no one to help us, and at our rate of progress a book of 300 pages would take at least two years to produce."
Regarding James Joyce, *Ulysses*

The pain of not hearing

Sometimes not getting any response to your material is more stressful than getting a rejection. If someone turns it down, at least you know where you stand. When you've sent something out weeks or months ago and heard nothing back, you feel even less in control.

Here's something you should know right at the beginning: Although there are exceptions, the publishing world and the broadcast and film worlds are not polite. In publishing these days, frequently if someone is not interested in what you're offering they won't give you the courtesy of a reply, even if you've enclosed a stamped, self-addressed envelope. I approached three publishers with the idea for this book. One, I am happy to say, contacted me very quickly, invited me in for a cordial chat, and offered a fair contract right off the bat. The second sent a form rejection letter months after I'd signed that contract. The third never bothered to reply at all.

Turning to television and film, Woody Allen once said, "Hollywood is the only place where you can die of encouragement." What he meant was that people almost never criticize an idea, they rave about it and convince you that they want to work with you forever and name their first-born after you. Once you're out of their office they never phone you again and refuse to take your calls.

I'm being very blunt about this for a reason, namely to remind you: Don't take it personally. This is how some of them treat everybody. Again, you don't need to find dozens of publishers or producers who are reasonable and fair and a pleasure to work with, you only need to find one (or, at least, one at a time).

The 25 beans method

Some time ago I read about how one of the motivational geniuses of the twentieth century taught salesmen to get over their fear of asking for business. He gave each of them 25 navy beans to put in the left pocket of their trousers. Every time they made a sales call, they moved one bean to their right pocket. They were not allowed to quit for the day until they'd shifted all of the beans. By focusing on the whole process, rather than on individual rejections, they were able to keep going. And invariably at some point in the day they made a sale, which motivated them to continue.

You can apply the same technique, without the beans. For example, if you're about to start submitting a novel, draw a "beans chart" with 25 squares on it. Each time you send your work out, cross out one of the squares—on the assumption that at some point you'll get an acceptance (and if not, you can always draw more squares).

Don't ignore constructive criticism

If you're lucky, you may get some constructive criticism along with a rejection. First, send a thank-you note to the person who took the time to give that to you. They will be delighted, because all too often they hear back only from writers arguing with them. You don't necessarily have to agree with what the person said, you're just expressing your gratitude that they cared enough to offer their comment. Your note needs to say only, "Thank you for your comments, I appreciate the fact that you took the time to make them. Perhaps we'll be more in sync on another project in the future." Even a rejection can be an opportunity to forge a link that may be more productive another time.

If you get the same comment from several people—let's say that your opening is weak, or that your story sags in the middle—that may be a good indication that it's time to make some changes before you send the material out again. Even if you decide that this particular project is too flawed to fix, you can learn how to do better next time. I've noticed that many of us (me included) tend to rush past our failures or disappointments. Instead of stopping and learning from what went wrong, we jump back into the fray as quickly as possible. Nobody likes to dwell on disappointments, but you may be missing a chance to learn. This isn't a hunt for who is to blame, and should not result in a guilt trip. The idea is to find what you can learn, with the emphasis on what you might do differently next time.

The curse of the inner critic

You can ignore outer critics; it's harder to ignore the inner critic, who often is the harshest of all. This is an inner voice or feeling ready to judge everything we do, quite often before we actually do it. The criticism can take many forms: self-doubt ("I'm not old enough/too old"); excuses ("It would take too much time"); procrastination ("I'll do it when the time is right"); and fear ("If I fail, I'll look ridiculous").

The inner critic is responsible for the fact that a lot of break-through ideas are never realized, that a lot of half-finished manuscripts languish in drawers. It is the key factor in writer's block, and also in most other kinds of blocks.

A technique that allows you to get to the heart of the problem comes from the field of neuro-linguistic programming. When you're ready to use this technique to transform your own inner critic, settle comfortably in a quiet place where you will have at least 20 minutes without interruptions and follow the steps overleaf.

Identify your inner critic

The inner critic can take many forms: a remembered voice (perhaps that of a parent or other authority figure); a visualization of failure; a sinking feeling in the pit of your stomach, and so on. What form does it take for you? If you're not sure, think back to a time when you undertook some writing-related task and doubts or fears got in the way. How did these doubts or fears make themselves known to you? Alternately, think about something you'd like to do, but haven't had the nerve to begin. What form do your fears take when you contemplate the task?

Decide what you want

Some people say they would like to get rid of their inner critic altogether. However, it can play a constructive role in helping you evaluate how things are going and correcting your course. Ideally, the inner critic helps you make an initial decision and then gives you useful, constructive feedback as you proceed. Unfortunately, more typically, the inner critic keeps criticizing or questioning your initial decision as well as forecasting a disastrous outcome.

Formulate a statement describing the relationship you want with your inner critic. You may want to change the name from inner critic to inner guide to help you start thinking in a different way. For example, your statement might be, "I want my inner guide to be a friendly, constructive source of positive as well as negative feedback." Consider for a moment how it would feel if your inner guide did function this way.

Bring it into view

Where does your inner critic seem to be located? In your head? In your heart? In your gut? Perched on your shoulder? Wherever it is, bring it into view or awareness by picturing it going from its usual position to a few feet in front of you. To do this, turn it into an image even if normally it's a feeling. Play with the distance. If it's too close for comfort, move it further away. If it's too far away for you to feel connected to it, move it closer. What does it look like? Some people visualize their inner critic as the face of a particular person, others see a dragon or other animal, others see a blob of a certain color. If you don't get an image immediately, take a deep breath, relax, and let your imagination loose. Don't dismiss any images that come to mind.

How does perceiving your inner critic this way affect how you feel about it? What are you aware of now that you didn't realize before? Some people have a "Wizard of Oz" response. That is, they see that their inner critic is not as all-powerful as it likes to pretend.

Find the good intention

Usually the inner critic has a positive intention (just like those friends of yours who are negative). Often it is trying to save you from criticism or disappointment. After all, if you don't finish that novel, nobody will ever reject it. What is your inner critic trying to do for you?

Find an alternative

How can you attain that positive intention more appropriately? For example, can you have a trusted, constructive writer friend look over your novel before you submit it? Usually there is a more constructive way to achieve what the inner critic is trying to do.

Experiment

When your inner critic expresses itself, how do you feel? Quite often we relate to our inner critic the way a child relates to a stern adult. If this applies to you, consciously look at and listen to your inner critic as the adult you are. How does that change its effect on you?

You can play with changing the image or the sound. If it's a shrill voice, try making it soothing. If it talks very quickly, try slowing it down. If it appears as a mass of color, change the hue.

Reform and practice

Having experimented, now decide in which form your inner guide is most likely to be a helpful partner rather than a hindrance. Imagine it that way. Picture a situation in which you are considering undertaking a new writing project or task, and imagine how your transformed inner guide would help you: When would it appear; how would it look, sound, and feel; and what kinds of useful things would it communicate to you?

When you have the version that seems to be the way you want it, reinstall it. You don't have to put it back in the same place you found it. If it used to crowd you too much, keep it somewhere more comfortable.

For most people, this creates a helpful long-term change. If your inner critic makes a comeback, just do a 30-second review of the reformation. It will not be long before your inner guide is speeding your progress rather than holding you back.

KEY POINTS

- As a writer you can't avoid rejection, but you can learn how to handle it well.
- A rejection is just somebody's opinion.
- The harshest critic usually is your inner critic. Using the NLP technique in this chapter, it can be transformed into a constructive inner guide.

EXERCISES

- Take the time to identify your inner critic. If it is sometimes harsh and sometimes constructive, what makes the difference?
- If you get depressed by receiving a rejection, imagine yourself looking back on this day from the future. How long before this one rejection will seem insignificant? A week? A month? Try to remember what was upsetting you a year ago today. If you can't remember, is it likely that you'll remember today's pain a year in the future?

CHAPTER BONUS

On the website www.yourwritingcoach.com, click on the "Chapter Bonuses" tab, then the "Inner Critic" tab, and type in the code: guide. You will be taken to an audio NLP visualization that will help you build your confidence.

13

The Write Time

"One of the great acts of bravery is to go slowly. In the world of publishing and entertainment, I see products being ruined and audiences being short-changed by a false emphasis on speed. In fact, the best books are those that take their own time… The real challenge is to make products as beautiful and as individualistic as possible."

—Harriet Rubin

I wonder whether your experience with time management books and programs has been like mine. I bought the books, the forms, and the calendars, used them for a week or two, then fell back into my old time-wasting ways. This changed only when I realized that no particular technique would work until I addressed the much bigger issue of my *patterns* of time use. If you are not making the best use of your time, the problem may lie in the patterns of how you use your time, too.

In this chapter, you'll learn how to recognize patterns that may be holding you back and how to establish new ones that will make it easier for you to spend your time in ways that help you reach your writing goals.

First, a few basic points that will give you the context for these techniques:

- *People have patterns of behavior.* Not surprisingly, doing the same thing again and again results in the same outcomes again and again. For example, someone may keep having different relationships but always with the same kind of person, or someone may repeatedly get into money problems by misusing credit cards. Of course, there are also positive patterns: for example, certain people always land a good job or always drive safely. People have certain patterns for how they use their time, too. For example, some people will always tackle first the task they think will be easiest, while others start with the one they think will be most difficult.

- *More surprisingly, people tend to repeat their old patterns even when the outcomes aren't positive.* In other words, people don't necessarily learn from their bad experiences that maybe it would be a good idea to do something different (a little later we'll look at why this is). Therefore, it's not unusual for people to use inefficient or unproductive time patterns for years.

- *People tend to be aware of other people's patterns, but not their own.* It's unlikely that you will change until you are aware of your patterns. Once you know what they are, it becomes easier to change them, and therefore to change the outcomes.

- *Patterns can include feelings, thoughts, and images as well as actions.* For example, if you get a rejection letter, your next step may be to remember all the other rejections you've had, then you might remember the voice of your father telling you that you'll never amount to anything, then you might picture getting rejections in the future for the project you're currently working on, and then you may go get drunk to try to blot out all these negative thoughts and feelings. That's a disempowering pattern. An empowering one might be to receive the rejection slip, remember other times when something that was initially rejected went on to sell, go get the listings of other markets to which you might submit the rejected piece, and send it out again.

Discovering your own patterns

Here are some of the most common dysfunctional patterns relating to time use:

- Doing the least important work first.
- Procrastination.
- "Fire fighting" (doing what is urgent rather than what is important).
- Letting your inner critic dominate your thoughts.

How can you open our eyes to your own patterns? First, be clear why you're doing this. It's not so you can beat yourself up even more about your failures. You're doing it so you can figure out what you can do differently in order to get better results. So, with that in mind, here are six different approaches to discovering your own patterns:

- *Ask other people.* You can see their faults, so guess what? They can see yours! But you have to convince them that you want them to be honest, and you have to be sure that you can hear this kind of blunt honesty without endangering your relationship. If you start to feel bad about what you're hearing, just remember that this is the first step of change. It may be uncomfortable, but you're doing it so you can move forward. If several people recognize the same pattern in your life, they're probably right. Good questions to ask are: "What do you notice about how I use time? When do you see me using time wisely? When do you notice me wasting time?"
- *Consider what negative patterns your parents had and assess whether you may be duplicating them.* It could also be that as part of your rebellion against your parents, you became caught in a pattern that is the opposite of a parent's pattern, but that is also negative (e.g., "trust no one" turns into

"trust everyone"). In terms of time use, your parents may have had the pattern of putting things off until it turned into an emergency, or they may have been such perfectionists that they never had time to do all they wanted to do.

✐ *Think about a situation in which you'd like to understand your behavior better.* Imagine seeing yourself in that situation as though it's playing out on a movie screen with you as one of the actors who can be observed. This is the dissociated state, in which you're watching yourself as though on a screen (as opposed to seeing things through your own eyes). If you are truly dissociated, you won't have any particular feelings about what you're observing—no guilt, embarrassment, or anything else. You're just watching to find out what you can about this pattern. For example, if you have started and then abandoned several writing projects in the past, review exactly what happened.

✐ *Use the "teach your problem" technique.* In this, you pretend you have to teach someone how to behave the way you do. You have to give them exact, detailed instructions. For example, let's say the situation you're looking at is why you never seem to get any writing done on the weekends, even though that's always your intention. How do you manage to do that? To teach someone to replicate your behavior, you might instruct them to make promises to their spouse, partner, or children that involve the weekend. You might teach them to let minor tasks go during the week, so that by the weekend they absolutely need to be done. You might instruct them to stay up late on Friday and Saturday nights, so they don't actually get up until noon on Saturday and Sunday. You can write down this detailed curriculum, or you can speak it into a tape recorder, or if you're brave you can do it with another person being the "student" and let them take notes for you.

✐ *The next time you go through a pattern, map it as you go.* For example, let's say you decided you'd go to the library to do research for your historical novel on Saturday. Saturday comes around and you never make it to the library. As it happens, take notes about the process that causes you to change your mind. For example, maybe you get up and notice that the laundry has really piled up. You decide to put it into the washing machine and then go to the library. But as the washing is being done, you think you might as well give the house a quick tidy. Just as you finish and are ready to go out, your best friend phones. She's upset and needs a shoulder to cry on, so you sit there and listen to her latest romantic misadventure for an hour. Now you're hungry, so you make yourself a late lunch… Writing down a pattern as it happens often is enough of a pattern interruption that it will cause you to go ahead with what you originally intended—so this can be a curative exercise as well as a diagnostic one.

Whichever techniques you use, you may not be able to figure out every tiny step of the pattern, and that's all right. What is important is to get some idea of the main steps so that you have something to work with.

Understanding what your current pattern gives you

One of the assumptions of neuro-linguistic programming is that every behavior has a positive intention. It's trying to give you some benefit. One example is writer's block. Usually, the positive intention of writer's block is to protect the writer from rejection.

When you've identified a pattern, it can be useful to identify what it's giving you. Normally, it will be some kind of protection, often a protection from needing to face change, which is uncomfortable initially and sometimes very scary indeed. Even though this protection also has negative side effects, it's the devil you know.

Let's look at a few more examples:

⬦ The person who keeps putting off clearing out his "junk room" in order to create a writing space may be afraid of having to throw away items that have sentimental value because those items give him comfort. By avoiding the task, he gets the payoff of continuing to draw comfort from those items (just knowing they are there may give him this).

⬦ The person who intends to submit a manuscript for publication but never does may fear the same kind of ridicule she got when she was the overweight girl in the PE class, and by never letting an editor judge her work she gets the payoff of avoiding ridicule. Naturally, this kind of ridicule is unlikely even if the material is bad, but we're talking here about emotions, not logic.

⬦ The person who wants to make a career change but never moves toward it gets the payoff of not having to risk rejection.

There are some simple patterns that may not have a deep payoff, they may just be bad habits that you've fallen into. These should be easy to change. However, when you confront a set of behaviors that are not easy to change, it's worth investigating the payoff. Again, please note that the point of this is not to get down on yourself for your behavior, but rather to use it as a starting point for change. Let's see how this works.

Finding better ways to get a similar payoff

When you have identified what the payoff is, you can generate alternatives for getting the same benefits in more benign ways. When I work with people who have writer's block, I help them build protection from rejection into what they're doing, and that has always broken the block. For example, I might suggest that they make a pact with themselves to finish the project, with the proviso that they can then decide whether or not to submit it to anyone. When they've completed the project, we identify one person they feel safe showing the material to. When that person has given them feedback, they can decide whether to show it to others. At every step, they remain in control and protected. When they finally send the material to an editor or an agent, I always have them start on a new project right away, so their emotional focus is on that one, not on the one that may be rejected.

Here's the key point: It's not enough just to change your pattern, you must change it in a way that also gives you the payoff that was provided by the old pattern. If that element is missing, the new pattern is unlikely to last very long.

The person who avoids clearing out a junk room could consciously choose several items to keep for sentimental or comfort value and get rid of the rest. Or, as someone in a recent workshop mentioned as their own strategy, he could load the surplus items into boxes and put them in the attic instead of throwing them away. That way, they'd still be there if he wanted them. If they're not needed for a year or two, he may then feel secure enough to throw them out.

The person who fears getting ridiculed by an editor can test the material first with a supportive reader or writing group.

The person who wants to start a new career but is fearful of failure can break the process down into safer chunks. She may be able to try out her new skills in the context of volunteer work, where there is less pressure. For example, a writer could initially write articles for the newsletter of a charity organization, or could write children's stories and give out copies in a children's ward at a local hospital.

The key is finding what works for you, and it's a trial-and-error process. Please don't expect that the first thing you try will be the perfect solution. Approach the whole thing in the spirit of play and experimentation. Think of yourself as a social scientist researching what works—or, if you prefer, as a hero or heroine on your own journey of learning.

Use what already works

One of the best ways to find possibilities for changing an ineffective pattern is to look for times when you already do vary it.

I once worked with a writer who said she was "always" late for meetings. Naturally, this didn't endear her to editors, agents, or others who had to wait for her to show up. A closer examination showed that there was an important exception: She never missed a plane. Obviously, she employed a different pattern when she had a plane to catch. We figured out what she did differently at those times, which she can now also do in other situations when she's supposed to be somewhere by a particular time.

Here are some other situations where this approach works:

- If you generally procrastinate, what *don't* you procrastinate about?
- If you generally don't write down ideas that come to you, but once in a while you do, what's different about those times?
- If you generally don't finish what you start to write, but once in a while you do, what's different about those times?

In the exceptions to unproductive patterns, you will find clues to change. Quite often, the problem contains the seeds of its own solution.

Watch what you say!

All of the strategies above are based on the idea that you accept responsibility for your actions. I'm sure you're not one of those people who try to blame someone else for everything negative that happens to you, but are you using language (to yourself, if not to others) that suggests you are somehow powerless over your behavior? For example, some people say, "I can't seem to find an agent, no matter how many letters I send out." A more accurate statement would be, "I haven't yet found the right technique for attracting an agent for my work."

Instead of saying, "I can't write good descriptions," you might say, "I haven't yet learned to write descriptions as well as I'd like to."

Instead of saying, "I can never find the time to write," you could say, "So far, I've considered other things more important than writing."

This isn't a matter of just trying to sound positive for its own sake, it's really about speaking in a way that accurately reflects the choices you have. Language doesn't just reflect behavior, it influences it, too, so it might be interesting for you to monitor how you talk to yourself about your writing and your use of time. Compare it to how you talk to yourself in those areas you feel are going well. Generally, we're willing to take full responsibility for those things we do well, but are inclined to express less power over those things we've not yet learned to do well.

The power of saying "no"

One final major pattern to consider is that of saying "yes" to whatever people ask you to do. John Tudor has pointed out, "One of the reasons Shakespeare managed to write so many plays is that he didn't have to answer the telephone." Also, presumably Will's friends didn't come to him when he was in the middle of writing *Hamlet* and ask him to put together a little speech for them to give at the Red Cross Banquet—"You know, something funny about giving blood."

It's nice to be nice and to do favors for people. Just remember that every minute you are doing those things is a minute you're not writing. I'm not suggesting that you turn into a Scrooge who never does anything for anyone else, just that you value your time enough to be selective about what you take on.

Saying "no" also applies to saying it to yourself and considering other ways of doing what you do. There are three useful questions you can ask about the things that take up your time:

- *Is this really necessary?* For example, it's pleasant to have ironed sheets, but will your world collapse if you just fold them? It's great to stay in touch with friends, but does that mean you have to go to the cinema with them every Friday? It's quite relaxing to watch television, but isn't your book or article or short story more important to you than watching the latest antics on *Big Brother*? It's good to stay informed, but could you divert an extra 15 minutes a day from reading the newspaper or magazines?
- *Is there a faster way to do this?* If you're the family cook, opting for the microwave a day or two a week can be a great time saver. If you're the family bill payer and you're used to doing this once a week, maybe you can switch it to every two weeks or once a month. With many tasks the preparation time (in this case, organizing the bills, finding out which of your children has taken the calculator, etc.) takes as much time as the actual work. Whenever possible, consolidate tasks.
- *Can someone else do this?* This is my favorite question because whatever it is, it still gets done, just not by me. In some cases, money is the answer. You want the garden to be neat and tidy but you're not crazy about gardening? Hire a young person to mow the lawn and pull the weeds. Do the same with cleaning: Get someone to come in for half a day a week to do the hoovering, dusting, and laundry. If you have children, you're used to paying a baby-sitter when you want to go to the cinema. What's wrong with hiring one for two or three hours a week while you go to the library to write in peace? Allocating some money for these sorts of things is no different from spending money on anything that gives you or your spouse or partner satisfaction and pleasure. If they spend money on playing golf, buying CDs, or a gym

membership, you have the right to "buy" yourself some
quiet time during which you can write.

Of course, it may be that money is tight. If so, it's quite likely that
you have children. Well, from now on, make them work! If
they're past the toddler stage it's time they learned the economic
facts of life. There is no free lunch. Let them wash the car, help
with the cleaning and laundry, and mow the lawn. If they're old
enough to handle knives and the stove, let them make dinner
once a week. True, these jobs won't be done as well as if you did
them yourself, but is that so important? If you let them get on
with it after a bit of guidance at the beginning, they'll get better.
Someday maybe they'll thank you for teaching them the meaning of responsibility. Then again, maybe they won't. Who cares?
It won't have killed them, and you'll have gotten some writing
done.

Once you have uncovered your patterns of time use and
started experimenting with changing them, you will find that
suddenly things are changing for the better. Then it is much easier to integrate new time tools into your work. There are three I
have developed that my clients and I have found particularly
useful.

Time pods

By using what I call "time pods," you can drastically improve
your productivity even when you have a limited period in which
to work.

First, set aside one hour of time in which to achieve a particular task. This could be writing an outline, drafting a chapter,
interviewing someone, or anything else. Be sure you have all of
the materials you need, so that you won't spend any of this time
looking for a file or a stapler or a phone number.

Write down exactly what you intend to achieve in this time
period. For instance, "I will write five pages of my novel," or "I

will clear my email inbox of 50 old messages," or "I will use the internet to get the key dates I require for Chapter 2 of my historical novel." Please actually write this down, rather than just thinking it.

Next, set an alarm or buzzer for one hour. Get on with your task, and when the alarm goes off, stop. On the same sheet of paper, write down any observations or notes that might be useful in helping you to be more efficient next time. For example, you may have realized that there was something you needed in order to do the task that you didn't get ahead of time, but next time you can. If the hour was particularly productive, note what made it so.

If you have another hour available, before you move on to your next time pod take 15 minutes off and make sure to use at least five of those minutes for physical activity. If you're in an office, going up and down the stairs a couple of times is a good choice. Also allocate at least five minutes for some mental stimulation (e.g., browsing a magazine). Finally, be sure to take a big swig of water—many of us are lightly dehydrated much of the time and that affects our energy levels.

By giving each hour of your working time such a clear focus and recording what works and what could be improved, you will find yourself working with laser-like concentration and getting far more done that you used to.

Keep an accurate record of your phone calls

Creative people often have trouble with keeping track of the more mundane aspects of business. If you are phoning editors about assignments, or setting up interviews, or discussing projects with an agent, it is very useful to have an accurate, dated record of these conversations.

Jotting this all down on random slips of paper fits with the image of the absent-minded artist, but it isn't very effective. Instead, buy some "While you were out" pads from your local stationery store. Rather than using them for missed calls, fill one out every time you make or receive a phone call. Jot down the name of the person, the date, and the gist of the call, including any agreed actions. You can then file these by date, or at the end of the day file them by project.

Going MAD

It's true, as the Chinese say, that the journey of a thousand miles begins with a single step, and that most large goals are reached little by little. However, it's also true that sometimes we feel we are making so little progress that it's tempting to give up. Those are the times when using the MAD strategy is helpful. MAD stands for Massive Action Day. As the name suggests, this is a day when you devote yourself exclusively to taking massive action toward a goal in order to jump-start or restart your progress. Here is how to prepare for and conduct a MAD:

- *Focus on one goal at a time.* The idea is to make major progress toward one specific goal. If you have lots of goals that might benefit from massive action days, schedule them as separate events.
- *Put the day into your schedule well in advance.* Treat it as you would any other extremely important appointment—not as something that can be forgotten if something else comes up. If you feel that assigning a whole day will be too difficult, you can start with a MAHD—a Massive Action Half Day.
- *Be sure you have all of the necessary materials, tools, and supplies ready at the beginning of the day.* You don't want to squander the first hour or two rounding up the stuff you'll need.
- *Insulate yourself from interruptions.* This means turning on the answering machine and not taking any calls. If necessary, you can allocate 15 minutes at the end of the day to checking your messages and returning any calls that are

truly important. Explain your plan to anybody who might interrupt you and put a "do not disturb" sign on your door or near your desk to remind them. For some people, avoiding interruptions will be possible only by going to a totally different location to work (e.g., the library, a friend's house while they're out, etc.).

- *At the beginning of the day, note down everything you plan to accomplish.* Then prioritize the tasks and put them in the order in which you need to do them. It's a good strategy to use time pods, as described above. Take at least one short break every 60 to 90 minutes in order to keep your energy levels up. Have some healthy snacks ready (fruit is good, crisps and candy bars are not) and drink plenty of water.
- *When the time you've set for yourself to quit arrives, stop.* Take a few minutes to look back at the plan you set out and see how much you achieved. If there were obstacles, consider how you can prevent or overcome them on your next MAD. Recognize whether you underestimated or overestimated the amount you could achieve, and take that into account next time.
- *Reward yourself for what you've accomplished,* maybe by taking the time to do something enjoyable you haven't done for a while—going to a film, having a pampering session at a spa, listening to a new CD, or whatever works for you.
- *Consider whether another MAD would be useful* and, if so, pick a date when you can do this again.

You should find that a MAD will not only allow you to speed up your progress, it will also give you new energy in general. But don't overdo it—schedule no more than one MAD per week, otherwise the impact will be diluted.

When you have reformed your time habits and started using some of these techniques, you may find that not only are you writing more than before, but you are enjoying it more as well. It will feel less like a struggle and more like what we all want writing to be: an enjoyable, "in the flow" experience.

KEY POINTS

- The first key to making better use of time is to figure out your time patterns.
- When you work out the positive intentions of your negative behavior (such as procrastination) you can find a constructive way to get the same payoff, without the negative consequences.
- The language you use can have a negative effect on your behavior—or a positive one.
- One of the easiest ways to find more writing time is saying "no" to unnecessary activities.
- Using time pods, Massive Action Days, and a simple plan for keeping track of your phone calls and activities are three powerful time-saving techniques.

EXERCISES

- Set aside a half hour this week to review your time patterns and brainstorm more constructive alternatives.
- If you want to kick-start a writing project, schedule a MAD or MAHD for some time this week.
- The next time you talk to anybody about your writing, monitor the language you use. If it's negative, make a conscious effort to change it.

CHAPTER BONUS

On the website www.yourwritingcoach.com, click on the "Chapter Bonuses" tab, then the "Write Time" tab, and type in the code: time. You will be taken to an exclusive interview with Mark Forster, the UK's top time management coach and author of *Get Everything Done and Still Have Time to Play, How to Make Your Dreams Come True*, and *Do It Tomorrow*.

14

Keep On Keeping On

> "One never notices what one has done, one can only see what remains to be done."
>
> —Marie Curie

One of the toughest challenges for a writer is to hang on in there when working on a large project, such as a novel or screenplay. Having the idea is tremendous fun, most of us enjoy getting started, and even more enjoy finishing, but it's that long stretch in the middle that's the problem. In this chapter, we'll look at some potent ways to keep yourself going in that difficult middle phase.

Ask yourself the questions of creation

This is actually something you need to do at the beginning of the project, when it is still shiny and new, so you can refer back to it as needed. It is asking what I call the "questions of creation."

✐ *What do I want the viewer or listener or reader to feel when they experience what I have written?* There may be a progression of feelings you want to elicit, as when you're writing a novel or screenplay. In a horror film, you may want viewers to enjoy feeling afraid and full of dread. In a novel about an abandoned child, you may want readers to feel sympathy for the main character. Even in a non-fiction book that is mostly informational, you may want readers to feel something as well. For instance, if you are writing a personal development book about how to use self-hypnosis, perhaps you want readers to feel more confident about their ability to create their own future.

- *What parts of the project are most exciting for me personally?* These elements usually are the quirkiest or most individual and therefore often the first to be eliminated because they don't fit an established pattern or norm. However, they also may be exactly the elements that could lead you to a breakthrough, and by writing them down now you help ensure that you won't lose sight of them as you work on the project.

- *What unique strengths do I bring to this project?* Focus on your strengths, not your weaknesses, and figure out how to allow the project to reflect those strengths. For example, novelist Elmore Leonard writes brilliant dialogue and creates wonderfully vivid characters, features that more than overcome his weakness at plotting.

- *Where does my intuition lead me in regard to this project?* To explore this, you have to shunt aside your logical brain and take some time to explore your gut feelings about the project. Never mind for now what your head says about the project, what does your heart say? Then check whether your head and heart are in alignment. For example, your head may say that a certain topic is really hot at the moment so you should write a book about it, but your heart may tell you that you don't have enough interest in the subject to enjoy devoting months of effort to it. It's when your head and heart are in agreement that you are most likely to follow through and enjoy the process.

- *What are ten reasons I can do this project successfully?* Usually our first impulse on having a new idea is to come up with ten reasons we probably couldn't do it, and if we run short, helpful friends and relatives are happy to chime in with their negativity. Consciously listing ten reasons why success is possible helps to counteract this habit.

- *When the critics review this project, what kind of raves will they give it?* Be as specific as you can—even sit down and write the review yourself. This will help you pinpoint the qualities that you will be going for as you actually write.

It's a good idea to get a notebook that you dedicate exclusively to this project, and you can write your answers to the questions of creation on the first few pages. If you get discouraged with the project at some point, go back and reread your answers and they will give you fresh energy.

A unique planning exercise

Another thing you can do at the start of the project, and repeat as needed, is an imaginary interview with yourself. Sounds a bit crazy, but bear with me, it's one of the most useful techniques in this book. Go somewhere where you will not be disturbed, take a few moments to get as relaxed as possible, close your eyes, and then imagine that you have already completed the project and it has been a huge success. Take a moment to enjoy that feeling of satisfaction. In this future, you are asked to give an interview to a journalist or a television or radio presenter (choose whichever sounds most enjoyable). This person is going to ask you a number of questions about your successful enterprise. Here are the key questions:

- What attracted you to this topic?
- What did you hope to achieve?
- What was the first step you took toward achieving this project?
- What was one of the obstacles you encountered?
- How did you overcome that?
- Who helped or supported or inspired you along the way? (This could be a real person, or a writer you admire, for example.)
- What was another obstacle and how did you overcome that one?

- What was one of the first big milestones that showed you were well on the way with this project?
- What was the most enjoyable part of writing it?
- When did you realize that you were definitely going to be able to finish the project?
- What advice would you have for anyone else setting out to do something similar?

Your logical brain may be protesting that you can't possibly know the answers to these questions at the start of a project, but your subconscious mind, the source of your intuition, always knows more. You may be surprised at how easily the answers come to you. To make the process easier, you may want to tape record the questions, leaving enough time for your answers, so that you don't need to look at these pages. Alternatively, you can download an MP3 version of this exercise from the website, www.yourwritingcoach.com.

You can use a tape recorder to record your answers, remembering always to speak in the past tense since in this interview you have already finished your work. That way you don't have to stop to take notes. You can transcribe the recording afterward. That will give you a road map of the project, complete with some anticipated obstacles and strategies for overcoming them.

You can repeat this exercise whenever you feel stuck or your energy is flagging. In that case, make up your own questions about how you overcame whatever problem is besetting you at the time. For example, your imaginary interviewer might ask, "Halfway through writing the novel, you began to have some doubts about its value and were tempted to give up. How did you overcome that so you were able to complete the novel?"

Use metaphors to get past obstacles

There has been a lot of attention lately on the power of story-telling and metaphors in business, but using them is also an interesting approach to dealing with personal challenges. Here's a simple four-step process I've devised:

1   Pick a challenge or problem.
2   Create a metaphor for how you're handling it or how you're thinking of it now.
3   Create a metaphor for how you'd like to be handling it or thinking of it.
4   Decide what you'd have to do in order to act in a way that fits the new metaphor (and then do it!).

For example, at one point I had deadlines very close together for delivering a feature film script, a television film script, and the manuscript for a book, and it was causing me major stress. The image that came to mind—a visual metaphor—was someone who had three heavy sacks on his back, each sack representing one of the projects. Even when I was trying to focus on one project, the others were still weighing on me. I created a new metaphor, namely an image of three separate rooms, each one containing one of the projects. When I was in one of the rooms, the other projects were out of sight. In order to fit this new metaphor, whenever I worked on one project I kept all the materials relating to the other projects out of sight. It may sound strange, but it released the stress I'd felt and allowed me to work on these projects one at a time with focus and energy.

Talk nicely to yourself

A lot has been written about what we can learn from top athletes. One of the most revealing classic studies was described in *Scientific American Mind* magazine. The study revealed that athletes who qualified for the Olympics had the same levels of anxiety and doubt as their less successful peers. The difference was that the Olympians were better at continually encouraging themselves.

The key to performing well may be what you say to yourself when you doubt your ability to perform. It can be useful to remember past victories, remind yourself of your strengths, and look at others who are succeeding and tell yourself that if they can do it, you can do it, too.

Use potential regrets

A study written up in the *British Journal of Health Psychology* reveals that when students were asked how much they intended to exercise in the coming week, they were more likely to indicate a strong intention if they were first asked about how much they would regret it if they didn't exercise. If they were asked about their intention first, and then how much they'd regret it, they expressed a lesser intention. In other words, at least on the level of intention, it works better to consider first how guilty you'd feel if you don't do something, and then decide what you can do to make sure you don't actually experience that guilt.

When you're planning your day, move ahead in your imagination to the end of that day. What would you regret not having done? Then decide what you need to do in order to feel good at the end of the day. Then write down what you intend to achieve that day.

If you have trouble sticking to your intentions, start the week by sending yourself an email that briefly describes what you plan to accomplish that week. At the end of the first day, open that email, check off the planned tasks you've done, add whatever new tasks came up, and resend it to yourself. Repeat daily, and at the end of the week you'll have a record of what you meant to do and what you actually did. Print that one out. After a few weeks, you'll have a good picture of how well you're sticking to your plans—and what's distracting you if you're not.

Change your physical and mental state

I'll bet that sometimes you just don't feel like writing. Instead of giving up or sitting there and staring into space, change your physical state. Speaker and author Peggy van Pelt described how this works for her:

> "At certain points in work I'd have to get up, move around, or go do the dishes. But while I was doing those things, ideas would come into my head and I'd go back to the computer and finish whatever I'd started. For me, movement triggers the flow of ideas."

One especially useful form of movement is the cross-brain exercise. Kay McCarroll, of the Educational Kinesiology Foundation, says:

> "Movements on one side of the body will stimulate activity in the opposite brain hemisphere. By activating both sides of the brain alternately, you are building up and balancing the neural connections between the two."

Here's a simple exercise that experts say centers the brain, improving logical thinking, focus, and reading. Make a V-shape with the thumb and forefinger of one hand. Place it in the center of your chest, just below your collarbone. Rub this spot for 30 seconds while placing your other hand over your stomach. Exchange hands and repeat.

Certain scents also can help you change your mental state. One that has been found to be effective is the smell of peppermint. I keep a little bottle of peppermint oil handy and have a sniff when I feel I need to perk up. And if all else fails: caffeine!

What to do if you get stuck

Sometimes your lack of motivation doesn't have anything to do with your mental or physical state, it comes from feeling frustrated that there is a writing problem you can't solve. For those times, I have six strategies for you to put into practice:

- *Go back.* The problem probably is rooted in what has gone before (or what has not gone before). What could happen earlier that would make this moment more interesting, more challenging, more suspenseful, more funny, or more whatever you want it to be? Sometimes this means going right back to the characters, not only to the previous action. If you have miscast a character, fire him or her (as Elmore Leonard does) and hire a new one.

- *Think about what makes a party more interesting* and consider whether that might be what will make your scene more interesting as well. The options include:
  - introduction of a new character
  - introduction of a different emotion (of course it must be motivated)
  - introduction of new information (that has emotional implications)
  - open out subtle conflict
  - a subtext that goes counter to the text
  - a dramatic change in the environment
  - a realignment of loyalties
  Consider whether any of these would help make your scene more lively.

- *Try the "opposite" technique.* What would happen if your story went in the opposite direction? (Of course, you'll have to justify this, but don't worry about that at first.) You can also try this with characters: What if it's a woman instead of a man; a young person instead of an old one; a foreigner instead of a local; a neurotic instead of an assured person?

⊘ *Question your inner guide* as to the nature of the problem and the solution.

⊘ *Ask your characters what should happen next.* In your imagination, step into each character and write a page or two about what's on their minds, their feelings, and their notions of their future. This is also a useful exercise if there is one character you feel you don't understand as well as the others, or who is not coming alive on the page.

⊘ *Before you go to sleep, give your unconscious mind the request for a solution.* The next morning, recall your dreams to check if one appeared in them; if not, do a bit of brainstorming to see what new ideas come up.

I hope this chapter has given you lots of ideas for how to stay the course when you have undertaken a major project. Do come back to it from time to time, especially if you feel your energy flagging. It's important that you keep going so eventually the world will be able to share your creations. I'll leave the last word to Tom Clancy:

"Success is a finished book, a stack of pages, each of which is filled with words. If you reach that point, you have won a victory over yourself no less impressive than sailing single-handed around the world."

KEY POINTS

⊘ For each of your writing projects, keep a notebook in which you answer the questions of creation, and refer to it if your passion for that project starts to flag.

⊘ An imaginary interview in which you pretend to have completed a large project already can help you plan the steps to achieving it.

⊘ Changing your metaphor for a problem or challenge can help you solve it.

⊘ Changing your self-talk can improve your performance.

EXERCISES

✐ If you have a large project coming up or are already embarked on one, get a notebook and record your answers to the questions of creation.

✐ What is the biggest challenge you face at the moment? Come up with a metaphor for it. Then try changing the metaphor to one that is less stressful and notice the difference. Sometimes the new metaphor also contains within it a clue to a solution to the problem.

CHAPTER BONUS

On the website www.yourwritingcoach.com, click on the "Chapter Bonuses" tab, then the "Keep On" tab, and type in the code: keep. You will be taken to an exclusive video interview with NLP practitioner and life coach Alice Mallorie, in which she reveals the most successful motivational tools she uses with her clients.

PART IV

SELL!

"You must not only have the idea, but must also believe in it so strongly that you're not going to take no for an answer."
                                                           —*Marcian Hoff*

Samuel Johnson reportedly said, "No man but a blockhead ever wrote, except for money." I don't agree with that, but naturally we'd all like to be rewarded for our efforts. Whether or not this comes as welcome news, it's true that these days more and more of the marketing effort falls to the writer. In this section you'll learn the traditional skills that are still important, such as writing an appealing book proposal or query letter. But those are no longer enough; that's why you'll also find a chapter on innovative, effective marketing techniques that very few of your competitors will be using. You also have to understand what's happening in the marketplace, and the most important development underway now is the decline of the old media, such as newspapers and network television, and the rise of the new media, such as internet sites, blogs, and interactive games. In this part you'll find a chapter on how to turn this trend into an opportunity rather than a threat. Finally, the book concludes with some useful advice on how to have a long and successful career as a writer.

15

Marketing Yourself

"The man with a new idea is a crank until the idea succeeds."

—*Mark Twain*

For a time you could hardly open a publication of any kind without reading praise for the iPod (yes, I have one). But most of them focused on the styling, the ease of use, the permutations that keep appearing, and they missed the real genius of the entire concept. Namely, that Steve Jobs was able to get the record companies and artists to agree to a download service when "download" was a word they associated with piracy and loss of control. The iTunes site launched with about 200,000 songs and now offers over a million. I mention this because so many creative people feel their work is done when they're only halfway there: when their book is written, or they've come up with the idea for a film, for example. It's only real when it's getting into the hands of the end user; when—as Jobs did—you've overcome the doubts of the skeptics and enlisted the cooperation of those who can help you get your project out there and make it useful.

Most writers I have encountered hate the idea of having to sell themselves and their work. Is that true of you? What projects have you left half done? Maybe a few rejections put you off, or somebody's negativity convinced you to abandon the idea. Often it's the things closest to our hearts that we leave unfinished because we fear the pain of failure. Is it time to go back to that one "crazy" idea or project and get to work to make it come true?

If marketing yourself scares you, I have one thing to say: You're going to have to get over it. More than ever, the ability to sell yourself is a crucial skill for the writer. The good news is that, like any other skill, it can be learned. In fact, in this chapter and the next you're going to learn all you need to know about this process. After that, it's just a matter of practice. So if this subject strikes fear into your heart, I'm going to take you by the hand and guide you through it.

The process has several components, including the ability to "pitch"; that is, to tell people enough about your story or idea to get them to commission you or to ask to read the manuscript or script. This is usually the aspect writers find most daunting, so we'll get it out of the way first. The next is to do a pitch on paper, in the form of a query letter to an editor, publisher, or producer. As you'll see, this is very similar to a verbal pitch, it's just written down.

The pitch or query letter is enough to get you an assignment to write an article, or to get someone to ask to read your short story or novel manuscript or screenplay. However, if you want to get a commission to write a non-fiction book, the publisher will want to see a full proposal, so I'll explain what that should look like.

There is an old saying in sales, "Sell the sizzle, not the steak." That means showing people what makes a product exciting, rather than just telling them what the product is. When someone buys an expensive red sports car, he (and it usually is a he) is not buying a vehicle to get him from point *A* to point *B*, he's buying an image. That's the sizzle. These days we writers are working in an ever more competitive field, so we have to sell the sizzle, too, not only about our project but also about ourselves. Therefore, I'll be showing you how to present yourself in a manner that gets people excited about working with you.

This chapter covers the accepted, traditional, and still useful ways of marketing yourself and your work. These are necessary, but sometimes they're not enough. That's why I've included Chapter 16, which covers creative and effective ways to go beyond the usual techniques in order to really stand out in the marketplace.

Do you need an agent?

If you are writing articles, poetry, or short stories, you don't need an agent. In fact, most agents won't even handle those areas. If you're writing books, you don't always need an agent, but you will find it beneficial to have one. The one type of writing for which an agent is absolutely necessary is screenwriting. There are few studios or production companies that will look at scripts or ideas that are submitted directly by a writer. This is partly because they assume an agent will take on only writers who have a reasonable level of skill, which cuts down on the number of unsuitable scripts the studios or companies have to read. It's also for legal protection, because an agent will keep track of when material was submitted and to whom, which is helpful information in fending off frivolous lawsuits from paranoid writers who believe their material has been stolen.

What does an agent actually do?

Many writers assume that the most important thing an agent does is negotiate a good fee for your writing and make sure you are paid the royalties you are owed. That's certainly one element of their function, but even more important is their awareness of who is looking for what. They spend a lot of time socializing with buyers, following the trade press, and making phone calls. It's important to remember that they are not there to motivate you, lend you money, edit your work, or be your friend. Some do make editorial suggestions, usually in an effort to make your work more salable. It's a professional relationship and agents are looking for clients who behave that way.

How much do agents charge?

Most agents charge 10 to 15 percent of what you are paid. They may charge more for foreign sales, as in that situation they may be splitting a commission with another agent in the other country. They may also charge you for expenses directly relating to submitting work on your behalf, such as postage, photocopying, printing, and so forth. Reputable agents do not charge a reading fee, and I strongly encourage you not to do business with any who want to charge you for editorial services, or who say they will represent you only if you use the editorial services of their colleagues.

How do you find an agent and do you have to sign a contract?

Probably the best way to connect with an agent is in person. Many writing conferences invite agents and allow participants to have brief meetings to pitch their projects. Even if you don't talk to the agents, seeing and hearing them give a talk or participate in a panel discussion can help you get a sense of whether they might be a good fit for you. Another strategy is to find out which agent represents writers you admire. Often authors mention their agents in the acknowledgments sections of their books, or in interviews. You can also ask writing colleagues, writing instructors, and editors with whom you've established a working relationship.

There are listings of agents in a number of books and directories. In the UK, these include the *Writers' and Artists' Yearbook* and *The Writer's Handbook* (both of these are annuals, so be sure you have the most recent edition). In the US, agents are listed in the *Literary Marketplace*, which is available at most larger libraries, the *Writer's Market* annual, and Writersmarket.com, a subscription website. There's also a useful list on the website www.aar-online.org. In most cases, entries in these directories will give you an idea of the types of writers the agents handle, how large the agency is, how long it has been established, and its website. It's always worth going to the agency website to get the latest information. This is a business with many personnel changes, and you don't want to be addressing your submission to an agent who doesn't work there any more.

Agents may want to have you sign a contract just for the one book or project with which you approached them, or they may ask you to sign a one-year contract that would cover all of your work during that time. Be sure to read the fine print carefully and if there is anything that is confusing, ask. If there are terms and conditions that seem unfair to you or that you don't agree with, you have the right to ask to strike those from the contract. That may or may not be a deal breaker, but certainly you don't want to be tied to a contract that you consider is not in your best interests. Naturally, if you have signed a contract with an agent, during the term of that contract you will not be able to have the work represented by anyone else.

Is it okay to send out multiple submissions to agents?

It can take a long time to hear back from an agent, and I don't think it's reasonable to expect you to sit around for six months hoping for a "yes" only to get a "no" after all that time. I believe it's acceptable to send a query letter or a book proposal to a number of agents. If it's a novel or screenplay and the agent then wants to read the whole thing and says it will be done within a reasonable time (four to six weeks), then stop sending out material to others and wait for that response. If you're lucky and get several agents wanting to represent you, congratulations! Have a chat with each one, ask how they plan to market your work, and pick the best for you. If the others are upset, they'll get over it.

What if you don't have an agent?

Quite a few publishers do consider books or proposals submitted directly by authors. The same annuals I mentioned above list publishers and what they are looking for, as well as submission guidelines. Check the publishers' websites to make sure that the information is current.

If you are writing short stories, poems, or articles, you can approach publications that use that kind of material. Again, the annuals have information on a huge variety of publications, as do magazines like *Writing Magazine* and *Writers' News* (UK) and *Writer's Digest* and *The Writer* (US). Needless to say, you should look at several copies of a publication to make sure that what you're offering is in sync with what it wants.

Whether or not you have an agent, much of the work will fall to you. One of the key skills you will require is the ability to pitch, or verbally present, your material.

The power of the pitch

Come on a little fantasy with me. You step into an elevator, bound for the 35th floor. Just before the doors close, someone else gets in with you, glances at the buttons, and nods—they also are going to the 35th. You look at this other person and gasp. It's a very important person, an editor or producer who is exactly the target market for your work (henceforth referred to as the VIP). You would sell your grandmother to have this person buy your book or direct one of your scripts. The VIP looks depressed. You work up the courage to ask what's the matter.

The VIP says, "Oh, I just can't seem to find a project worth my time. I'm desperate—you don't have anything I might want to buy, do you?"

Narrowly avoiding fainting, you say that as a matter of fact you do have a manuscript—does the VIP want to read it?

"Tell me what it's about first," the VIP says. "Then I can decide whether or not to read it. You have until we reach the 35th floor."

Uh-oh. You begin, "Well, it's about this man, he has a great life in most ways—a happy marriage, two lovely children, a good job, you know, something in the City, he makes a good living, and his health is fine, too." You're already passing the 10th floor and the VIP's eyes are starting to glaze over just a tiny bit. "But he has a problem—by the way, his name is Bob Finster, and he's in his mid-30s. Or late 30s. Or even 40s, depending on casting, because in the movie version this would be a great part for a star. I was thinking Bruce Willis originally, but maybe he's a little too old now... Russell Crowe would be good, but I hear he's temperamental. Anyway, Bob has this problem..." Twentieth floor, and the VIP is looking more depressed than ever.

I won't take us all the way to the 35th floor, but I trust the point is obvious. Producer Stephen Cannell said it best in an interview I did with him years ago: "A good idea, badly presented, sounds like a bad idea."

You may be thinking it's not too likely that you'll be having an encounter in a lift with the VIP any time soon, and that's true. However, it's quite likely that if you're making any effort at all to get people to read your work or listen to your ideas, you will be encountering agents, editors, or producers. And in every case, before they actually read anything you've written, they will want to hear what it's about, either in a brief verbal pitch or a letter that's the written equivalent of a pitch. If that's not compelling, you've hit the end of the trail.

So what are the secrets of making an effective pitch? Here are eight crucial guidelines:

- *Let them know what kind of story you're talking about.* If I tell you that my story is about a man whose mid-life crisis motivates him to do all the things he never did in his mild youth, that could be a comedy—but it could also be a drama in which he endangers his marriage and career. If you start by telling the other person the genre, if it's a comedy they will be listening for what makes the story funny; if it's a horror story they'll be listening for what will provide the chills.

✐ *Hook them before you provide any back story.* In the lift example, it would be far better to start by saying, "The main character, Bob Finster, is a man in his mid-30s who is missing only one thing in his life." That makes your listener wonder what this one thing is. Now you can briefly tell him a few of the things Bob is not missing—"he has a great wife and kids, a lucrative job, his health is good"—and then you can satisfy the VIP's curiosity by revealing what Bob is missing.

Let me give you an example from my own experience. Some time ago, I was pitching an idea for an American television film about the second wife of President Woodrow Wilson. The first time I pitched it, I started at the beginning:

> The story opens in the White House in 1915. Woodrow Wilson is in office, and his wife has just died…

It didn't take long for the listener to lose interest (people in Hollywood have the attention span of a gnat). I revised the pitch to this:

> These days, the notion of a woman president isn't a question of whether, but of when. Maybe it'll be Hillary Clinton, maybe it'll be Condoleezza Rice, or maybe it'll be someone we haven't heard of yet. But actually we have already had a de facto woman president. This woman made appointments to the Cabinet. When the Queen of England visited the United States, this woman caused a scandal by refusing to curtsy because she felt she was of equal stature. She took on Congress for several months— and won. She was Woodrow Wilson's second wife, and this is her story.

This opening sparked the listener's interest; then I was able to back-track and tell the story from the start. This was a longer pitch; if it had been an elevator pitch, I would have shortened the teaser to, "Did you know that America has already had a woman president?" Of course, I would have had to qualify that a bit, but it's definitely an attention getter. In case you're curious, I haven't sold the project—yet. I've put it back in the drawer, to be pulled out the first time a woman gets nominated for the presidency.

- *Make your characters individuals.* You don't have much time to describe your main characters, so you have to be concise and colorful in providing a mental image of them. In something I've written recently, a character named Bloom is a bit of a con artist, and I'd describe him as short, overweight, and always sweating a little. You don't have time to do this for all your characters, just the main two or three. The others will have to be described by their functions—the landlady, the taxi driver, the lonely neighbor. Don't give everybody names, because it takes too long and it's hard for the listener to remember who's who.

- *Get to the meat of the story fast.* It's tempting to spend a lot of time on the set-up, the call to adventure—the beginning (in scripts this is Act One of the three acts). Generally, Act One is fun, but it's in Act Two, the middle, that we find the meat of the story. It's also where most manuscripts and scripts and ideas fall down. In a brief pitch (or letter) you don't have time to go into all of the developments of your story, but you should tell three or four major developments that escalate the conflict, and you certainly will want to include the "moment of truth" at the end of Act Two, the highest point of crisis. (If any of these references are confusing to you, you probably haven't read Chapter 9, about structure, so it might be a good idea for you to do that now, and then come back.)

- *Don't leave out Act Three, the ending.* Some people think it's cool to leave the listener hanging, the idea being that if they want to hear how the story comes out, they will have to buy the manuscript or script. Wrong. Too many stories have illogical or otherwise weak endings, so your listener wants to make sure that yours will not.

- Weave your theme into your story. If the story includes a theme or lesson, try to incorporate it in your story naturally rather than stating it separately at the end. I've already referred to the classic film comedy *Tootsie*, in which Dustin Hoffman plays a failed actor who disguises himself as a woman in order to get work. In a pitch you could include a statement something like this: "Ironically, it's only as he experiences being a woman that he begins to understand how to be a better man. Now he's ready to find true love with the woman he works with—but he can't reveal his real identity without losing his new success as an actor." The first statement is the theme, the second relates it to the plot.

- *Tell your story with enthusiasm.* When I was publishing the *Hollywood Scriptwriter* newsletter, I asked the agents, producers, story editors, and studio and network executives the same question: "What is the one most important quality of a good pitch?" Unanimously, they said enthusiasm. If you don't sound like you really believe in your story, why should they believe in it? If you are an introvert, as many writers are, find a way to show your enthusiasm that feels comfortable and natural. This can be as simple as putting an extra bit of energy or warmth into your voice.

- *Practice!* If you do a bad pitch in a workshop, or in front of your spouse or partner, or your dog, or the mirror, no harm done. You want to make your mistakes before you are actually talking to someone who can help (or hurt) your career, so practice as often as you can.

Once you realize that pitching is really just another version of what you love to do—telling stories—it loses its power to intimidate.

The query letter

The query letter is just the written version of a verbal pitch, with the advantage that you can take your time over it and hone it until it does a great, concise job of sparking the reader's interest. If you are proposing an article, the reader will be an editor at a magazine; if you are seeking representation, it will be an agent; if you are trying to sell a screenplay, it will be a producer or network executive. Here is an example of such a letter:

> Dear Agent [Naturally this would be the name of a specific agent]
>
> I would love to have the opportunity to send you a copy of my novel, a thriller called "The Devil's Choice."
>
> The story opens in 1945. Deep in the Philippine jungle, there's a small hut with a dirt floor. A prisoner is collapsed in the corner, beaten nearly to death by Japanese interrogators. Donald Trent is one of a elite group of 12 American soldiers, caught during a night drop that went horribly wrong. When his captors realize Trent knows about the secret weapon being developed by the American government, they give him a terrible choice: Reveal what he knows, or Japanese agents in America will kill his entire family.
>
> Trent gambles the future of his country by telling what he knows—but then leads his men in a daring escape and a harrowing pursuit of the messengers hand carrying the secret of the atomic bomb to the Emperor in Tokyo.
>
> In the showdown inside the city itself, Trent sacrifices his life, but eliminates the threat to his family and ensures that the secret of the atomic bomb dies with him.

Although the story is fiction, I have based many of its elements on historical fact. I spent six months in Japan, researching this era and the Japanese spy services during World War II.

If you would like to read "The Devil's Choice," please return the stamped, self-addressed postcard I have enclosed, or contact me via phone or email. I look forward to hearing from you.

Sincerely,

A Writer

Let's take a look at the elements in this letter. The first paragraph tells the genre of the novel and its name. The second creates a dramatic image in the mind of the reader, introduces the protagonist, and sets up his central conflict. The third paragraph summarizes the crucial elements of the middle of the book. Naturally, one short paragraph can't begin to cover all of the exciting adventures the writer might have in mind for this part of the book, but there's enough there to whet the appetite. The next paragraph reveals the resolution of the story, including the fact that the protagonist sacrifices his life. The one after that reveals information that gives credibility to the writer, namely that a lot of research has gone into this story. The final paragraph wraps things up and indicates that a stamped, self-addressed postcard is enclosed.

This is a concise and effective model that you can use for any query letter you write when you have a finished work you'd like someone to read.

Next, overleaf is the query letter that I wrote for the book you are reading now:

Dear (Publisher)

I suspect if you had a penny for every time someone said to you, "I'd write a book if I only had the time," you'd be a richer man. These people are the target audience for the book described in the enclosed proposal. It's called "Your Writing Coach," and actually it will appeal both to would-be and practicing writers. As you'll see, it covers motivation, writing short-cuts, and the most important psychological aspects of writing, as well as specific time management techniques for writers.

I am the co-author of *Successful Scriptwriting*, published by Writers Digest Press, which sold more than 65,000 copies. My most recent book, *Do Something Different*, is in its second edition from Virgin Books and has been translated into Chinese, Spanish, Korean, and Bulgarian, and sold a special run of 8,000 copies for the Institute of Chartered Accountants. I am also a successful scriptwriter, with credits that include *Family Ties*, *Benson*, *Love Boat*, *Relic Hunter*, and many other series and TV movies.

I hope this manuscript will be of interest to you. I have enclosed a stamped, self-addressed envelope, and I look forward to hearing from you.

Sincerely,

Jurgen Wolff

In this case, the query letter was accompanied by a full proposal for the book, so the letter was short. It began with a question that I hoped would capture the attention of the reader. I was confident that anybody in the publishing field hears the "I'd write a book if I only had the time" comment at least once a day, so I felt this would be a good opening. The paragraph then gives a very brief indication of the book's contents; just enough, I hoped, to lead the reader to the fuller proposal.

Almost half the letter refers to my publishing history and experience as a writer. For non-fiction books, it's important that you have relevant expertise. If you've had some success selling books in the past, that also is important to mention because it instills confidence that you will do it again.

Query letters for articles

If you are proposing to write an article for a magazine, you would write a similar letter. Your first paragraph might start with a "hook," a statement that grabs the reader's interest right away. For example, for an article covering a new approach to helping people quit smoking, it might be, "The average success rate for hypnotists who try to help people quit smoking is 63%. Dr. Franklin Arbuthnot's success rate, independently verified, is 95%." The rest of the paragraph might summarize his innovative approach, and reveal that the doctor is willing to give you his first interview ever about his technique. You might also mention two medical experts you plan to have comment on his work, and that you will supply photos of clients undergoing this treatment. Your second paragraph would give your background, including publications that have carried your work in the past. You could also include a couple of clippings of your previous work, so the editor can see your writing style.

Query letter dos and don'ts

When you write letters like this, make sure that any experience you mention does relate to the project you are proposing. I've seen letters in which writers have cited irrelevant academic achievements or skills and even their hobbies. This is a waste of valuable space and also is distracting.

It's important that these letters go to a named individual, not just to "The Editor," and that the name be spelled correctly. If in doubt, always check first. Most publishers, agencies, and production companies have websites that include the names of their key employees or at least a contact telephone number. Don't hesitate to ring a company and say, "I'm sending a package to Mr. X, and I just wanted to double-check the spelling of his name."

Try to keep your letters to one page. Editors are busy people, so the more you can give them the vital information in a precise and concise form, the more they will appreciate it.

What goes into a book proposal?

If you are trying to sell a short story, a first novel, or a screenplay, potential buyers will expect you to have written it all before you approach them. So much of the value in a work of fiction is its execution, not just its idea, that they generally want to see the whole project in order to evaluate it. Once you've had some success as a fiction writer, you can switch to getting commissions for further books or scripts based on pitches or query letters.

However, for non-fiction books, the standard procedure is to submit a book proposal. The components of the proposal are:

- A *query letter* like the one above.
- A *title page* with the name of the book, your name, and your contact details.
- A *table of contents* for the proposal itself.
- An *introduction* that serves as an overview of the book you are proposing. This would include why you think the book is needed, how long it is, how far along you are in writing it, how long it would take for you to deliver the completed manuscript, and any special features it will offer.
- *Markets for the book*: who your target buyers are, and why they will find this book appealing.

- *Promotion:* how you will help promote the book. This is becoming more and more important. Publishers' promotion money is stretched and frankly quite often it goes to their already successful authors. If you can show you have concrete plans for making people aware of your book, that will be very appealing to a publisher. In this context, you may run across the term "platform" or "author's platform." What this refers to is your ability to spread the word to people who are already aware of you. If you have a popular e-bulletin or newsletter or podcast, for example, or you address big groups every year, you have a platform. If you don't have one, your proposal should indicate how you would go about establishing one. This doesn't mean you have to be famous in a general sense, only in the area you are addressing in your book. If it's a gardening book, then you have to show how you will become known within the world of gardening fans.
- *Competitive and complementary books:* a brief look at what similar books are out there already, how successful they have been, and what is different about your book. By the way, you might think if there are no other books out about your topic this will be a hot selling point. The truth is almost the opposite. The publisher will think if there's never been a book on this topic, that's probably because there's no market for it. If loads of people are already buying books about this topic there is a strong market, and all you need to do is appeal to these people with a different angle of some kind. The best example of this is diet books: There are hundreds of them, yet new ones appear every year.
- *About the author:* your relevant background and experience, your previous publications or productions, and where you are based.
- *List of chapters* and summary of their contents (one or two paragraphs for each chapter).
- *Two sample chapters.* These don't have to be the first two chapters, they can be from anywhere in the book. Naturally,

you want to choose two that are strong in terms of their appeal, so if your book offers something new or different, pick the two chapters that best exemplify this. If a chart or other illustrative material is essential to the chapter, enclose that, too. These chapters should be typed just like the rest of your material.

How long the proposal is depends on how long your sample chapters are. A typical book proposal might run between 20 and 50 pages, double spaced. You can see a full sample proposal on the website www.yourwritingcoach.com.

This chapter has covered the traditional marketing techniques used by writers. There are also more innovative and creative techniques that can augment these and set you apart from the mass of other writers. You'll discover what these are in the next chapter.

KEY POINTS

- Writers have to take the main responsibility for marketing their work.
- It's essential for you to be able to do an "elevator pitch"; that is, a colorful, brief, verbal summary of what your project is about.
- A query letter is the written-down form of a pitch.
- To sell a first novel, you have to write it all. To sell a non-fiction book, you need to write a book proposal.

EXERCISES

- If pitching makes you nervous, practice by creating a pitch for the most recent film you've seen and the most recent book you've read. The process is less intimidating when the material is not yours.

✐ Try your pitch out on different people and gauge their reaction. You can test a few different opening statements, for example, to see which one makes people most curious.

✐ When you've written a query letter, read it out loud. That may expose weaknesses for you to address.

CHAPTER BONUS

On the website www.yourwritingcoach.com, click on the "Chapter Bonuses" tab, then the "Pitching" tab, and type in the code: pitch. You will be taken to a video interview with top UK agent Julian Friedmann, of Blake Friedmann Literary Agency, who reveals what agents look for when they consider representing a new client.

16

Guerrilla Warfare for the Writer

"Be daring, be different, be impractical, be anything that will assert integrity of purpose and imaginative vision against the play-it-safers, the creatures of the commonplace, the slaves of the ordinary."

—Cecil Beaton

In the previous chapter we looked at the traditional ways of marketing yourself and your work. All of those methods are fine, but in a highly competitive marketplace they may not be enough. These days it's useful to consider yourself a brand and to plan to promote that brand. The first step is to give careful consideration to what sets you apart from other writers.

Find your strategic focus

When you are first establishing yourself as a writer, it makes sense to figure out your niche and stick to it. If you hop from novels to film scripts to poetry collections, for example, you are splitting your energy and effort into three parts. That's fine if you want to write as a hobby, but if you want to have a career it means you're only exerting 33 percent of your available energy on each genre. It takes a lot of work to establish yourself in any market, so it's a good strategy to pick one and focus your efforts on it. If you feel that giving up the others will stifle your creativity too much, then do those in any spare time you have left.

Presumably you have already identified your niche by reading Chapter 2.

What's your USP?

Within the niche you have selected, what is your USP? USP stands for unique selling proposition, and it means the aspect of a product or service (or the person providing the service) that sets them apart from the competition. An article in _International Artist_ magazine suggested that it's just as important in the art world. Art consultant Graeme Smith wrote:

> "When I was running my own gallery we tried to identify the USP for each artist we represented... the more we cemented the USP in the minds of our clients, the more easily they were able to remember each artist and their work."

Here is Smith's advice on how to identify your USP:

1 Write down everything you do that is characteristic of you or your work.
2 Now go through your list and cross out all those points you have in common with other artists (or others in your profession).
3 What you have left is your USP. If you have crossed everything out, you need to consider what you'd like your USP to be and then work toward it. Smith advises, "Don't allow yourself to be sidetracked—you must be persistent... without [a USP] you are lost, you won't even get noticed."

If you are writing crime novels, what is different about them? If you're offering a cookbook, what sets it apart from all the others out there? What is it about your short stories that makes them memorable? Do you already have a USP? It can be useful to ask people who are familiar with your writing what they think your

USP is, and find out whether you are being perceived the way you'd like to be.

The likability factor

How well you write is the most important element in your success, but don't underestimate the importance of how you deal with people. In his book *Blink*, Malcolm Gladwell points out that people never sue doctors they like. There is a strong correlation between the doctor's warmth, the interest they take in the patient, and the amount of time they spend talking to a patient, and whether or not they will ever be sued for malpractice. *The Science of Influence*, by Kevin Hogan, reveals a similar phenomenon among real estate agents. One of the strongest factors in whether buyers buy from a real estate agent, he says, is whether that agent expresses interest in the client. Hogan's advice: Sell the client on *you* first.

In your writing career you will be dealing with agents, publishers, producers, publicists, and members of the public. If you handle them in a manner that makes them want to work with you, you will easily double your chance of success. Some people have a natural warmth and ease, but some are shy, which can be misinterpreted as aloofness or even arrogance. How can you make a good impression? The following are some of the strategies and techniques that Hogan suggests:

- Give direct answers to questions and elucidate how that information will help the other person solve their problem. This is another way of saying: Always focus on what *they* need, not on what *you* need.
- Given the choice of being brief and simple or long and complex, be brief. Show other people your flexibility and allow them to stay in their comfort zone.
- Always give something of perceived value, with a personal touch if possible. This doesn't mean bribe the person with

something irrelevant; in my case, it might mean leaving behind a copy of my book, for example.

Standing out in this regard is not difficult. If you treat people with courtesy, take an interest in them as well as in yourself, have respect for their time, and thank them when they do something for you, you will already stand head and shoulders above the crowd.

Your new mantra: Do something different

My book *Do Something Different* includes 100 case studies of how individuals—authors and others—have creatively marketed themselves and their work. The principle behind all of the stories is that if you do what everybody else is doing, you get what everybody else is getting. For writers, this means lots of rejections. If you do something different from what the crowd is doing, you and your work will stand out. You'll have a greater chance of being noticed and therefore also a greater chance of being successful. I suggest you write the phrase "Do something different!" on an index card and tape it to the wall near your desk so that you will always be reminded of this concept.

Below are some examples of how writers and other creative people have applied this idea.

Don't take "no" for an answer

M.J. Rose wrote a first novel called *Lip Service*, but publishers rejected it because it was a mixture of genres—a thriller crossed with a love story, crossed with a bit of erotica—and they couldn't figure out how to market it. Rose took matters into her own hands. She set up a website and started selling digital copies of the book. Then she self-published it in a run of 3,000 copies and spent long hours online, finding websites to which to send the book and asking for reviews. After three months of effort, she had sold 1,500 copies and it was the highest-ranked small press novel on Amazon. The Literary Guild picked it as a featured alternate selection—the first time it had ever done this with a self-published novel. Conventional publishers took notice and Pocket Books won a bidding war for the hardcover and paper-back rights.

Whether or not your book has found a publisher, how could you use the internet to locate an audience?

Create an alter ego

Jill Conner Browne was a single mother living in Mississippi, working as a fitness instructor and writing a humor column for a couple of regional newspapers. She developed the persona of a "Sweet Potato Queen," a brash, outrageous character who stood up for other women. After a radio appearance she was offered a two-book advance of $25,000. The result was *The Sweet Potato Queen's Book of Love*, which went through 18 printings, and *God Save the Sweet Potato Queens*, which sold 150,000 copies in its first four months.

Creating a character is a great marketing tool—would Jamie Oliver have become as famous if he hadn't started out as "The Naked Chef?" Your alter ego doesn't need to be outrageous, it could be "The Gardening Granny" or "The Birdman of Basildon," as long as it gives the media a catchy hook.

Find your audience

When Tony Fairweather, then managing a book club for the *Voice* newspaper, was told by mainstream publishers that they didn't target black people "because they don't read," he took it as a challenge. He started organizing three-hour poetry, music, and comedy shows built around black authors—and sold books by the hundreds. That was the start of his events marketing company The Write Thing. He features established authors with huge success: 1,000 hardbacks sold on the night Alice Walker was a guest. But he also promotes less well-known writers. "Writers are the stars of tomorrow," he told a London *Evening Standard* interviewer, "and we package them in a way people can identify with."

Could his efforts serve as a model for you? For example, instead of a traditional (usually sparsely attended) book signing, you could team up with poets and other entertainers to present an event at which your book is sold.

Play a stunt

First-time author Allistair Mitchell, who writes under the name P.R. Moredun, had rejections from seven publishers and 36 literary agents for his fantasy novel *Unearthly History*. Desperate to do something different, he commissioned model makers to fashion what looked like the foetus of a dragon with wings, talons, and a tail. He put it in a jar and told local reporters that a friend, supposedly the grandson of a porter from the Natural History Museum, had found it in a garage. The story was picked up by the national newspapers, and after that around the world. Only then did Mitchell confess to the buying manager of Waterstone's that it had all been a hoax. The Waterstone's buyer agreed to purchase 10,000 copies of the book. *Unearthly History* has sold well, and Mitchell's second book also has been published.

A hoax can be an effective way to get attention for your book, as long as it is relevant to your topic and is harmless. Naturally, in these days of heightened anxiety, it's important not to do anything that might frighten anyone. Leaving suspicious-looking packages for journalists, for example, is not recommended.

Train them to buy

Author Tanya Sassoon wanted to show publishers that there would be a market for her unusual product, "The Boyfriend Training Kit." It comes in a brown envelope and contains a small book of rules, another book for noting the boyfriend's offenses, yellow stickers to use as warning cards, and so forth. The training kit was part of her arts degree course and she made 70 copies to offer for sale at London's ICA Bookshop (which is known for selling avant-garde products). The bookshop accepted the copies, and sold out within a few weeks. This impressed Bloomsbury Publishing, publishers of the Harry Potter books, enough to buy the world rights to the product.

If you need to demonstrate the appeal of your book or other product, consider where you are most likely to find a receptive audience. If the experiment is a success, document it with facts, figures, and further evidence that you can use to make your case with other distributors.

Use humor to capture attention

Recent graduates Paul Gaye and Steve Reeves were hoping to secure jobs, or at least internships, at a major London advertising agency. This was at a time when a slowing economy had wreaked havoc in the advertising world, and there were few, if any, new positions open. Gaye and Reeves wrote an identical letter to every creative director in London (who were all men). In each case, the director received a letter written on pink, perfumed paper. The letter started: "Dear (Name of Director), You probably won't remember my name…" and alluded to a passionate evening in a car park 23 years before. The outcome of that night was twins: Steve and Paul. The letter finished with the statement, "They're trying to get into advertising and I hear you're quite good at that sort of thing." Enclosed was a Polaroid photo of the young men.

Only one director failed to respond; the others were appreciative and several wanted to meet the young applicants. One of the directors, Tony Cox, gave them a job and kept the letter on display in his office.

This effort succeeded not only because it was funny, but because it demonstrated the creativity that would be important in their field. If you use a funny stunt or ploy, make sure that it fits the nature of the book or product you're promoting.

Use the power of numbers

Seven crime writers who wanted to get more attention for their work formed a group called Murder Squad—with the tagline "Crime fiction to die for." They made their first public appearance at the opening of a Borders bookstore. They also printed a full-color brochure offering their services for readings, workshops, and talks at bookshops, libraries, and literature festivals. They have garnered considerable publicity and been invited to a variety of events at which they have promoted their books.

It's natural for us to consider all other writers as the competition, but consider whether there may be a way to work together in a win–win situation.

Give them a taste

The other surviving members of the Monty Python troupe were reluctant to let Eric Idle use their material for his hit musical *Spamalot*—until he gave them a sample. He told an interviewer from *The Times* (London):

> *"That was the hardest thing—to persuade them that this was something that would go well. We played them the song, 'The Song That Goes Like This,' and they cracked up. That was the secret of it."*

The show became a hit on Broadway and opened another production in London.

Publishers sometimes do something similar by offering readers a sample chapter of a book, either online or in print. You may be able to do something along these lines.

Consider what's in a name

Brenda Cooper had a lot of experience in overcoming rejection. In an article in the *Financial Times*, she wrote:

> "When I first started out in the music business, the reasons given for rejecting me and my work were, predictably enough, that I was too young and too inexperienced. Over the years, I've heard every reason why my music wasn't suitable for a particular project... These continual rejections took their toll on my confidence and my spirit."

She carried on writing because of the satisfaction that the process itself gave her. And she did something different:

> "I wasn't ecstatic about being called Brenda (not a cool name for a composer) but it wasn't until I changed it that I realised what a difference it could make. A producer in New York gave me the idea. He picked out my initials from my business card and said, 'B. B. Cooper, now that's a good name for a composer.' I began to use it immediately and couldn't believe how differently people treated me."

Since then, she's written for the stage version of *The Jungle Book*, formed her own publishing company, and released three albums on CD.

In most cases, using your own name will be fine, but if it's a bad match with what you're writing, consider using a pen name. For example, Bob Fotherington may not be a great name for someone writing sexy romance novels, and I've noticed that most action-thriller writers tend to have short, punchy names.

Sometimes size matters

Karl Fowler publishes big books—they measure 2 ft square, have 850 pages, weigh 90 lb (32 kg), and carry an equally hefty price tag: $4,000 (£2,000) and up. They are sports books, one about the history of the Super Bowl, another about Ferrari, another about Diego Maradona. They have a clear target audience: Fowler points out that Ferrari has more than 50,000 active members worldwide and there are six million cardholders for the Super Bowl. Some of the books include separate autographs and memorabilia. The books aren't sold in bookstores, but in posh department stores like Harrods and Saks Fifth Avenue.

If you are dealing with a unique topic, consider whether a special matching format might help your book to stand out.

Giving credit where it's due

Kevin Smith employed an unusual tactic to promote his film *Clerks II*. The first 10,000 people adding one of the film's MySpace.com pages to their friends list had their names included on the closing credits, on a horizontal scroll.

In this case, as with a young songwriter you'll read about in Chapter 17, a writer used his creativity to help fund his work. Could you do the same?

Sometimes free is good

I'm sure even if you're not a fan, you're aware of the Sudoku craze. Seemingly coming out of nowhere, this puzzle turned into a worldwide phenomenon. It was invented in the 1970s by an

Indianapolis architect named Howard Garns. Eventually it got to Japan where it was given the name Sudoku, and where a New Zealand puzzle fan named Wayne Gould spotted it. He wrote a computer program for cranking out Sudoku puzzles and rating their difficulty. Here's the part that's of interest to writers, as reported in *Time* magazine:

> "He also had a brilliant if counter-intuitive marketing model: give the puzzle away. More than 400 newspapers worldwide run his Pappocom sudoku puzzles free in return for promoting Gould's computer program and books. The results must be lucrative, as sales of the books alone have passed 4 million."

Is there a way that you might give away your product in order to promote another one?

Using a little of the creativity that you already employ in your writing will undoubtedly allow you to follow in the footsteps of the creative marketing people I discovered for this book, and with similar success.

Getting on radio and television

The best exposure you can get for your writing is appearances on radio and television programs. The media are monsters with a huge appetite. There are hours and hours of time to fill, so if you have something new and interesting you'll have a pretty good chance of getting your 15 minutes of fame. For instance, if you are writing a self-help book, there will always be programs interested in having you come on for a few minutes as long as you explore a new angle on the topic.

The secret is to find a hook, a one-line statement that makes what you are offering sound exciting. Let's say you've written a book on the joy of gardening. First, a non-hook:

Next we have an interview with Fred Bloggs about how much fun it is to garden.

Ho-hum. Now, a hook:

Next we have an interview with Fred Bloggs, whose survey shows that 56 percent of women prefer gardening to making love with their husbands.

It might be that this very unscientific survey represents 25 ladies who belong to a gardening club, but that doesn't matter, it will pique curiosity. The hook doesn't always have to be sex, it just needs to be something that makes people curious (for better or worse, sex seems to be the thing that makes people the most curious).

Remember that radio and television are made up of sound bites. You will not have half an hour to rhapsodize about the pleasures of peonies, you'll have three to six minutes and they'd better be good. This means you should practice until you can deliver half a dozen interesting bits of information quickly, and slip in the name of your book at least two or three times. For example, instead of saying, "The reason I wrote this book is…" I would say, "The reason I wrote *Your Writing Coach* is…"

Once you have identified the radio and television programs that might be interested in having you as a guest, ring to find out the name of the producer who books the guests. Then send him or her a query letter that includes the hook and a couple of sound bites—the sort of thing you'd actually say on the program. If they are interested, they will contact you and have a chat on the phone. No matter how informal this chat seems, it's an audition. They are checking to find out how articulate you are, how concise, and how entertaining. You have to be ready and give it your all even at this early stage.

Doing media appearances is definitely character forming. Years ago I was a guest on a national daytime talk show in America, *The John Davidson Show*. Davidson was a wholesome singer/actor, and I was given three minutes, sandwiched between a large woman demonstrating a Cajun recipe and John's solo singing spot, in which he warbled "Oh Mein Papa." The first thing that happened was that John totally mangled the question his producer and I had carefully plotted as the logical introduction to the rest of the interview. I managed to get us back on course, but I couldn't help feeling that for most of our little time together John had his mind somewhere else, possibly on trying to be sure he'd remember the second verse of "Oh Mein Papa."

On another talk show, this time a local one in San Francisco, the hostess was as sweet as honey before the program started. She assured me she'd enjoyed the book and that she thought I was brilliant (this should have alerted my suspicion, but Vanity, thy name is Writer). She patted my hand and told me to relax and pretend this was just a conversation between friends. When the camera's red light came on, she turned to me and said, in tones that suggested I belonged in the dock at the Nuremberg War Trials, "Why do we need another book on this subject?" There followed six minutes the likes of which hadn't been seen since the Spanish Inquisition. As soon as the camera turned off, all was sweetness and light again. I smiled bravely and thanked her for a most stimulating experience—after all, you never know when you'll have another book to promote.

I cite these two experiences to bring home a point: When dealing with the media, be prepared for anything. And whatever happens, remember to say the name of your book as often as you can fit it in.

I hope you've found these stories and case histories fun to read, but underlying them is a very serious point: If your book is to be successful, there is one person who has the main responsibility for making it so—*you.*

KEY POINTS

- Writers have to consider themselves a brand and promote that brand.
- You should identify your USP, your unique selling proposition.
- If you do what everybody does, you get what everybody gets. To stand out, do something different.
- Study inexpensive creative marketing techniques used by people in other fields and adapt them to yourself and your work.

EXERCISES

- Summarize your USP as concisely as possible. Does everything you do support this USP? If not, consider getting rid of the tasks or goals that don't.
- For each of the case studies in this chapter, brainstorm how the methods they used could be adapted for the kind of material you want to write.

CHAPTER BONUS

On the website www.yourwritingcoach.com, click on the "Chapter Bonuses" tab, then the "Guerrilla Warfare" tab, and type in the code: warfare. You will be taken to an exclusive interview with one of the mystery writers who belongs to Murder Squad. You'll hear how the group has capitalized on this identity and how any group could do something similar.

17

New Media, New Opportunities

"We're facing an unprecedented uncertainty in our lives. Living with uncertainty forces us to let go of attachments to how things should be. We'll have an excellent opportunity to practice inner flexibility, to look at our expectations and step behind them… The greater our personal creativity, the better we can ride through it."

—*Peter Russell*

The way we consume media is being turned upside down. Previously we were passive consumers, now we are active; previously we lived by the media's time schedule, now we can record or download programs and view them when we please; formerly we just consumed media products, now it's increasingly easy for us to create them as well; formerly there were few choices, now there is an almost overwhelming number; formerly it was difficult to give feedback to media producers and suppliers, now it's simple and instantaneous.

Keeping up with all of this is a challenge, and for writers it's also an opportunity. In her editorial in *script* magazine, editor-in-chief Shelly Mellot summed this up well:

"Business-savvy screenwriters are watching developments in new media and how those developments can translate to opportunities. For example, videogames are becoming more and more about the storytelling behind the game, making writers a hot commodity in that industry. DVD releases almost always feature extras about the production, extras which must be scripted. Even popular television shows

require extras to be produced for their DVD collection releases. Screenwriters are now being hired to write original content for cell phones, material developed for the Web, virtual reality, and interactive TV. All of these new outlets are creating jobs for writers to develop content and fill the new demands of today's consumers."

There are also additional channels for producing and distributing your writing, including websites, blogs, podcasts, and via print-on-demand books. The internet has made it possible for you to reach a worldwide audience. Although one challenge is making them aware of your work, the other is figuring out ways to get them to pay for it.

New media continue to evolve with amazing and sometimes alarming speed. Therefore, I'm going to give you an overview of the most important strategies in this chapter, and also direct you to the website (www.yourwritingcoach.com) where you will find regular updates on the newest developments and opportunities as they arise.

New media markets: Film and television

The studios are interested in films that will draw huge audiences, blockbusters that cost $100 million or more to produce and distribute. They are written by a handful of top writers. Small, independent films offer newer writers more of an opportunity, but until recently the market for such films has been limited. Many showed only in arty cinemas in major cities, so their ability to make money was minimal.

All that is changing drastically. The first step was the advent of DVDs and distribution systems like Netflix. These began to make it easier for people to see films that were not available at their neighborhood cinema.

The next, even more important step is the increasing ease with which we can download films over the internet. This is going to make it possible to sell or rent out films that may appeal to only, say, 100,000 people who are scattered around the world. If each of them pays $10 to watch that film, the film maker will have made $1 million. Given the staggering decline in the cost of shooting and editing a film on digital video, that's a large enough budget for an independent film maker to make a good movie. The big blockbusters will continue to be made by the large studios, but there is going to be a huge market for small films with niche appeal—and all of them have to be written by someone.

The same is likely to happen with short films and series. People are finding a ready audience for their short productions on YouTube and Google Video. Already some sites offer amateur video contributors a share of the ad revenue their videos attract. As Scott Woolley wrote in *Forbes* magazine, "Now a new type of video network promises to radically change what we can watch, who can create it, and who will profit." He quotes YouTube co-founder Chad Hurley: "Hollywood will always bring great content, but amateurs can create something just as interesting—and do it in two minutes."

A number of scripted television series have been created specifically for the internet. One of the first was *Broken Saints* (www.brokensaints.com), which utilized a partly animated graphic novel format, with 24 episodes of varying lengths. It concerned four strangers who receive cryptic messages leading them to their fate of saving the world. The series attracted 50 million visits to the internet and then was released on DVD. The first DVD release sold 10,000 copies, and more recently a four-disc box set has come out.

Another example is *Soup of the Day* (www.zabberbox.com), a sexy romantic comedy with 34 episodes, each three to eight minutes long. The first 19 episodes had approximately six million viewers, and also a DVD release. A spinoff featuring some of the same characters is in the works.

The third such program is *Floaters*, a series about three young female roommates working as temps at a New York ad agency while hoping for fame and fortune in show business. It appears in five-minute daily segments that then comprise one longer episode per week. The first season consisted of 15 episodes. The series is produced by Phoebeworks Productions and employs four writers.

Reflecting the legitimacy of this field, an Emmy Award category now honors new media programs. Journalist Christie Taylor writes:

> "Not since cable television has the industry experienced such a shift. Those willing to write for the Internet and portable devices now have the chance to gain recognition from the most respected leaders in the industry, and at the same time help shape the new cross-media form of storytelling."

The first year that this category was established, they had 74 entries, more than any other Emmy Award category.

One entrant was *Stranger Adventures* (www.stranger adventures.com), an interactive game/story produced by Riddle Productions. On the Writers Store website, Riddle development executive Richie Soloman revealed that they employ a mix of experienced and newer writers:

> "We have also hired writers who had no produced work and weren't in the [Writers] Guild, based strictly on the simple fact that they had a great story to tell. After all, isn't that what it's all about, telling a great story? Internet programming doesn't have the gatekeepers that traditional outlets like features and television shows have had. New writers have a greater chance of breaking in strictly based on their talent and not their relationships in the industry."

One of Hollywood's top five talent agencies is taking notice of this field by establishing an online unit devoted to scouting up-and-coming creators of internet content. United Talent Agency, which represents Jack Black, Vince Vaughn, and M. Night Shyamalan, wants to locate new writers and directors and match them with companies looking for people who can create material for the web. Brent Weinstein, head of the new UTA Online division, told *The New York Times*, "The barrier to entry is so low, everybody is now a potential artist." The agents will look at unsolicited submissions, preferably as web links.

New media's impact on publishing

The migration of consumers from print to new media has been dramatic. In 1892, London had 14 evening newspapers; now there is one (plus a couple of skimpy give-aways). In 1960, 80 percent of Americans read a daily paper; now it's more like 50 percent. Naturally, the money follows the consumers, and the internet is where they have been going. In early 2006, a Merrill Lynch report indicated that online media were about to overtake magazines in terms of advertising revenue. At this point, a lot of online content is sourced from print publications, but more and more there is demand for original content as well, both text and multimedia.

The UK regional publisher Newsquest has converted all 14 of its newsrooms into multimedia centers that will produce video content for its websites. The group owns papers including the *Glasgow Herald*, the *Oxford Mail*, and the *Colchester Gazette*. Margaret Strayton, Newsquest editorial manager, told *MediaGuardian*:

> "Like most other publishers we have accepted that multimedia, embracing all distribution vehicles for our journalism—print, digital, video, podcasts, mobile phones—is where the future lies."

It also lies with writers who can tell a story in a variety of ways for a variety of media.

The self-publishing option

Self-publishing has been with us a long time, but it has evolved greatly in the last decade. It used also to be called vanity publishing and had a bad reputation. Generally, it involved an author who could not find a commercial publisher for his (or her) book so he got a vanity publisher to print 1,000 copies and stashed them in his garage. He gave away six copies to relatives and friends, sold six copies, and the rest stayed in his garage for a few years until his wife made him throw them away. However, even before self-publishing started to change, there were some amazing success stories. For example, *The Celestine Prophecy* by James Redfield was first self-published. So was *Rich Dad, Poor Dad* by Robert T. Kiyosaki and Sharon L. Lechter. Both went on to be acquired by regular publishers and enjoyed enormous international success.

You can still go the vanity publishing route, of course. If you are a good marketer, it can make sense to have a few thousand copies printed and sell them yourself, especially if you deal directly with a book printer rather than a vanity publisher who will try to extract all kinds of extra fees from you. However, with the advent of digital printing and automated binding, there is now another alternative: print on demand. One of the most popular services doing this is lulu.com, established by Bob Young, the Blooker Prize man. You upload your manuscript to the site and when an order comes in for even just one copy, lulu prints that copy and dispatches it. It sets a minimum price based on the length and size of the book and whether it includes color, and you can decide how much above that minimum you want to charge. The difference is your profit.

A similar service is offered by Antony Rowe, the publisher used by writer John Howard for his novel for young people, *The Key to Chintak*. Howard received about 30 rejections from agents and traditional publishers before he decided to go the self-publishing route. He visited 40 schools with his book and the enthusiasm of the teachers and children convinced him that he had something that would sell. He went ahead and eventually both W.H. Smith and Waterstone's decided to stock the book. Since then he has had interest from several international publishers for the foreign rights and three film companies for a possible film version. By the way, Anthony Rowe has a very useful free print-on-demand manual that you can download from the website www.antonyrowe.co.uk.

The profit margins on books published by print-on-demand publishers typically will not be as high as those enjoyed when you print several thousand copies at a time; however, you also don't risk having your spouse threatening to set the garage on fire if you don't clear out all those moldy books you haven't sold.

My advice is start with a print-on-demand publisher and see what kind of response your book gets. Be sure that your contract specifies that the rights to your book and the files used to publish it remain with you. If it starts selling like hotcakes, you can either take it to traditional publishers who may be interested even if they rejected it before, or you can go to a regular book printer and get several thousands printed and continue to sell them yourself.

The biggest challenge for those who publish a book themselves is finding the audience for it. Most book chains will not stock self-published books, and most publications will still not review them (although, as you read above, there are exceptions, and there is a procedure for listing them on Amazon). This means you will have to find clever ways to market the book outside the normal channels. For inspiration, have another look at Chapter 16 and the unusual marketing ideas it contains.

The e-book alternative

An e-book, or electronic book, exists only as a data file until someone downloads it and prints it (of course, they can choose to read it only on their screen, as well). You can compose the book using a program like Microsoft Word, and then save it as a PDF document. It's easy to incorporate illustrations or photos, and the document can be just about any length. When people download it, they need Acrobat Reader to read it. Fortunately, this is a free program that most computer users already have (if not, they an easily download it from the Adobe website). You can charge people for the e-book download, using a payment service like PayPal or a credit card account, and the price you set is totally up to you. There are e-books that sell for hundreds of pounds or dollars, and many of them are shorter than traditional books.

The key, of course, is offering content that people feel they can't get anywhere else. The further advantage to buyers is that they will get this information almost instantly on clicking the "Buy" button on your site. There is no delay waiting for the book to be mailed to them. The advantage to you is that the amount you charge is almost pure profit. Other than the cost of main-taining your website, which you would do anyway, and possibly some fees associated with setting up a shopping cart on that site, and a small commission to PayPal or other payment service, you have no further expenses. With a traditional publisher you get 10 or 15 percent of the cover price as your share; with an e-book you net about 90 percent.

Again, the nature of the content is what will determine whether your e-book is a success. If, for example, I want to buy a book about training a dog, I'm not going to spend money (espe-cially more than a traditional book would cost) on an e-book I have to download and print out myself, when I can find dozens of relevant titles on Amazon or at my local bookshop. However, let's say that I have a Great Dane puppy, and your e-book is *The Secrets of Training a Great Dane Puppy in Ten Days*. If you con-vince me in the sales copy on your site that this e-book contains information I won't find anywhere else, I'm clicking that "Buy" button even if it costs me double what I'd pay for a traditional book, and that money will flow into your account instantly.

The best way to get a feel for e-books is to order a couple. I offer *Time Management for Writers and Other Creative People* at www.timetowrite.com, and you'll find e-books available at many websites you visit. Of course, once people have downloaded an e-book, it's easy for them to share either the download information or the file itself with friends. You can restrict the download period to a day or a week, so that at the end of that period the link goes dead. You can also create a PDF password system so that anyone who wants to open the book has to type in the password, to make it just a touch more work for people to share the file. However, my attitude is that most people are honest and the ones who aren't will figure out ways around your systems anyway.

You can also create e-booklets as well, or e-pamphlets, when you don't have enough material for a book, as well as audio and video files. On my site, I offer short reports for a small fee, e-books and audio tracks for a bit more, and multimedia programs that include CDs and DVDs for a higher price. All of these are new options for the writer, alternatives that extend our reach and allow us to provide information and entertainment with much more control than we used to have.

From real to virtual and back again: Opportunities in games

Even games are having an impact on publishing. Consider Second Life, a 3-D virtual reality world that has over one million "residents." Created by Linden Labs in 2003, it is an online plat-form on which members can build homes and businesses, chat with other users, listen to music, and shop. Second Life even has its own currency, "Linden Dollars", which can be converted to US dollars. Many businesses have established a Second Life presence, including the publisher Penguin. Within Second Life, users can find excerpts from Neal Stephenson's book *Snow Crash*, listen to audio clips, and buy the book at a discount. Second Life also hosts a much smaller publisher, Winged Chariot. Founder Neal Hoskins told *Guardian Unlimited*:

"I'd like to look for talent in here. I envisage starting small with something like a poetry or secrets wall where residents can leave notes about their Second Life experiences and then publishing the best of them… the book could even be brought back into the real world."

The gaming world is expanding into new areas, representing new markets for writers. The Federation of American Scientists has called for government-sponsored research into how gaming can be applied to education. Doug Lowenstein, president of the Entertainment Software Association, said: "We would be crazy not to seek ways to exploit interactive games to teach our children." Lowenstein cites the fact that there will soon be 75 million Americans between the ages of 10 and 30—the group that has grown up on video games, a huge target audience for games that teach as well as entertain.

An example of a game targeted to learning is "Brain Training," one of Nintendo's efforts to create new kinds of games that go beyond the traditional market. It is based on the book *Train Your Brain*, by Ryuta Kawashima, and represents an effort to come up with new games that do not require high-end graphics. *BusinessWeek Online* reported that Sony is also "at pains to persuade developers that they could benefit from a gameplay strategy that does not necessarily depend on massive resources."

This suggests that gaming may be a promising area even for writers who are not necessarily technically gifted. In any event, don't let the technology intimidate you. You don't need to understand the technical side of all these media in order to provide content, any more than you need to understand how a car engine works in order to learn to drive. Yes, a basic grounding will help, but you do not have to be a techno-geek to write for the new media.

The lesson of all this is that while the older methods of distribution will remain for projects with mass appeal, for the first time the new media have given writers an easy way to reach niche audiences. And it's not necessarily the case that a niche new media audience means small rewards, as the stories that follow will illustrate.

The opportunities are out there: Four inspirational stories

This first story, from the art world, illustrates how one person has found huge success that would not have been possible before the advent of the internet. As you'll see, it combines creative passion and skill with luck and adds up to a lot of money.

In 2000, British artist Jacquie Lawson created a beautiful animated Christmas card and sent it to a few friends. Then she left on vacation in Australia for three weeks. When she returned, she had 1,600 emails in her inbox. Her friends had passed the card along to other friends, who loved it and passed it on… and on. Jacquie Lawson's email address was on the card, and now all these people wanted to know whether she had other cards. She decided to turn her idea into a business. For $8 a year (£4.50 in the UK), you can send as many of her cards as you wish, from a selection that currently numbers 76. She has more than 300,000 subscribers. Have you done the math? That's about $2.4 million (£1.2 million) a year. Her renewal rate is about 70 percent, and she prides herself on not having to put ads on the site. If you want to see what the cards look like, go to her website: www.jacquielawson.com. If you consider that she is a 65-year-old widow who had no internet experience, you can see that there truly are opportunities out there for everyone!

Two London teachers have come up with Britain's first podcast revision course to help students prepare for business studies exams. The *Evening Standard* writes that the teachers had the idea when they noticed how many of their students have iPods or other MP3 players. They wrote the material, drafted friends to speak it, and recorded and edited it themselves. Now they are selling it to schools in the form of a teacher's CD and 20 CDs for students, or students can buy the course themselves. At the moment business studies is the only topic they have available, but they are planning to add other subjects. Clever thinking—and maybe a whole new market for writers.

The short story seems to be a dying art form, but maybe the mobile phone will bring it back. A young Japanese author who goes by the single name Yoshi distributed 2,000 flyers to teenage girls outside a Tokyo subway station, publicizing his story "Deep Love." The story itself was delivered via a mobile phone site he started, and he made payment voluntary. Facing the text limit of 1,600 characters that a mobile phone can hold, he wrote a tale full of eroticism and violence, using colorful, simple language. Its audience included people who normally didn't take the time to read books. Over the course of three years, his website received more than 20 million hits and his story was then published in conventional form, selling 2.6 million copies. Yoshi went on to write and direct a film version of the tale, and it became a television show and a Japanese-style comic book. His initial investment in the cards he handed out and his website? $1,000 (£477).

Aspiring British songwriter Jonathan Haselden came up with an inventive and profitable way to find patronage. He spent four months marketing his lyrics on eBay, selling lines from one of his songs to individuals and companies to use as they wish. They will also get a share of his publishing royalties from the single. The companies that bought lines include TGI Friday's, Taylor Guitars, Tussauds Group, and Budweiser Budvar. A US-based buyer paid £11,100 ($21,700) for the line, "And when you're lost, you'll be found again."

Content is still king

Sometimes it's easy to be dazzled by new technology and let it obscure the basic fact: Technology changes the way content is delivered, but without content there's nothing to deliver. Jeff Berg, chairman of top agency ICM, pointed this out at a meeting of the Wharton Business School undergraduate media and entertainment club. Of these new distribution formats he said, "all of them are new markets for us to sell into." He noted that consumers now devour about 35 to 40 hours a week of media, including television, music, games, and so forth. The emergence of new media also gives new value to old content because it can be relicensed into new channels. For instance, I've just discovered a website that is replaying episodes of *Moment of Terror*, a radio series for which I wrote when I was just getting started, more than 20 years ago (too bad my deal didn't include royalties!).

There is a lot of debate about whether and how people will pay for content on the new media, but if you consider that people are spending more than £2 billion per year for cellphone ringtones, you see that if you have something they want, they will pay. At this stage, the bigger question is *how* they will pay: pay-per-view, by watching adverts, by subscription, or via some other model.

If you want to be a player, play

If you want to get in on these writing opportunities, you have to be aware of what the new media are, how they work, and what they can do. This means actively involving yourself. For instance, if you think you might want to write for any of the games platforms (such as online games, Playstation or X-Box games, and so forth), you need to play the games, read trade magazines that cover this field, and, if possible, go to games conventions. That way you will find out which companies are most active, their policies regarding using freelancers, the correct formats for scripts for games, and all the other specific information you require to take part in this field.

If you want to write for websites, you have to explore the internet, find out which sites or services pay for content, and learn what kind of writing style works best on the web. If you find a site for which you might like to write, contact its owners and see whether they are interested. In this arena, there are not yet a lot of formal channels for applying for jobs or assignments, so be bold and just ask.

Do you have a website?

A recent survey shows that 60 percent of writers have a website. It should be 100 percent; these days having a website is like having a business card.

One example worth a look is the site belonging to veteran writer and broadcaster Clive James. A few years ago he established www.clivejames.com, which he describes as "halfway between a space station and a university campus." On the site you'll find his work in text, audio, and video sections, a gallery, and poetry by James and others. As he explains, the site is just part of a collection of outlets for his work, now that he is less involved with mainstream broadcast television. He is embarking on a new interview series on the satellite and cable Sky Arts channel (formerly Artsworld). James told the *Guardian*:

> "Artsworld have first dibs on transmitting as a cable channel and I can have the interviews on the web. I get a sum of money from them—which is not a large amount—and a sum from any other sell-on to, say, a cable channel in Australia called Ovation. Then there's Slate *magazine in the U.S., owned by* The Washington Post, *who are going to transmit the archive…"*

Some writers have multiple websites. I have one that is connected to this book, another (www.timetowrite.com) that focuses especially on time management for creative people, and another one (www.BrainstormNet.com) that is concerned with creativity and productivity. Naturally, they all promote each other as well.

If you have any traditionally published books, you can sell them directly from your site, or link to Amazon and other online booksellers. You will receive a small commission on every book that anyone orders via your site from Amazon or similar sites. If you have e-books, you can make them available for download from your site, and put on a PayPal facility that makes it easy for visitors to pay for what they buy. This is fairly simple to set up; see www.paypal.com for information.

Your website does not need to be all singing, all dancing. If you want to do it yourself, you will find that most hosting sites offer you templates that you can adapt fairly easily to contain samples of your work, a brief biography, and, most importantly, contact information for anyone who wants to reach you. If you wish to sell things from your site, it's not complicated to add a shopping cart and payment facility.

Are you blogging?

It seems that nowadays everybody and her brother has a blog, an online diary. Supposedly there is a new blog launched every second. The numbers are undoubtedly inflated because they refer to how many people start blogs, not how many keep them active once the novelty has worn off. Nonetheless, there are a huge number of blogs out there. They are easy—and many are free—to set up and maintain. The question is, are they of any use to a professional writer? The answer is, sometimes.

One example is the Blooker Prize, which goes to books that resulted from blogs. In 2006 it was won by Julie Powell, a 32-year-old New Yorker who used her blog to chronicle her attempts to cook all 524 recipes in *Mastering the Art of French Cooking*, written by celebrity chef Julia Child in 1961. Powell shared her reflections about cooking, love, and life. Then she turned the blog into a book, *Julie and Julia: 365 Days, 524 Recipes, 1 Tiny Kitchen Apartment*. The book, published by Penguin, sold more than 100,000 copies. In an interview with the *Guardian*, Powell credited blogging with kick-starting her writing career:

> *"I had no idea what a blog was a week before I began. The medium really liberated me and motivated me to do the work and not obsess over the details."*

A blog allows its readers to make comments and suggestions, which can be useful. Powell said:

> *"The community aspect of blogging and the interaction with others kept me honest, kept me writing, and kept me from sinking into my habitual self-loathing."*

American entrepreneur Bob Young, who sponsors the Blooker Prize, commented, "Blooks [books from blogs] are the new books—a hybrid form at the cutting edge of both literature and technology." In the past year, more than 100 bloggers have landed book deals.

On FastCompany.com, Leslie Taylor writes, "Blogging can be transformative—placing you on a new career path, earning you a book deal, or catapulting you into the field of your dreams." She cites Jeff Jarvis, author of the media and news blog BuzzMachine. He says:

> *"I left my corporate job to take the consulting gigs, speaking gigs, and writing gigs that have come my way as a result of the reputation I built up through my blog... It makes sense for people to discover talent this way. I've had people tell me they wouldn't hire [a writer] without reading their blog."*

Having a popular blog can also help point people to your website, where you can sell your books or other products. My blog, www.timetowrite.blogs.com, offers writing tips and gives me a chance to pass along interesting writing-related tidbits I come across in my reading. I also put on it little animated films I make as a hobby, and use it to remind people of my websites and what they offer.

When you create your blog, remember that there are two elements that will attract people (or not). One is whether you're offering content that they find useful in some way. The other is your personality. Don't make the mistake of thinking that your blog should sound neutral or authoritative and detached. You're an individual, so let your uniqueness shine through just as you do in person.

Your blog entries can be just about any length, but it's wise to chop them up into small chunks, ideally no more than 500 words or so each. Reading material on a computer screen takes effort and people will appreciate bite-size paragraphs. If you have several posts that cover a particular topic, you can always give them titles followed by "part one," "part two," and so on.

If you quote articles or materials, be sure to attribute the source. Copyright applies to blogs as much as to any other format. You can quote small segments of an article or book in order to review or comment on the source material, but if you want to include a significant portion, get permission first. In many cases the writer will be happy to allow this as along as you indicate where the quote came from and perhaps add a link to that person's website.

You will have the chance to allow or disallow comments to be added to your posts. Generally, it's a good idea to allow them, as this makes the blog more interesting and gives readers the feeling that they're participating, not just reading.

There are many blogging sites that allow you to set up your own blog in minutes. I use typepad.com, and blogger.com is also popular. Reporters Without Borders offers a useful *Handbook for Bloggers and Cyber-Dissidents*, which you will find if you put that title into your search engine.

The power of podcasts

Podcasts are like little radio shows that you record and put on the internet. All you need is a microphone, recording software (it's available free from audacity.com), and a computer. You then upload your recording to a hosting site, where it becomes available for people to listen to. They can also subscribe so that they are notified every time you add a new episode. One of the best hosting sites is iTunes, which is run by Apple but can host podcasts created with Windows software as well.

To get an idea of the wide array of podcasts available, go to iTunes.com and click on the "podcasts" section. You'll be able to see the various topic categories and sample as many podcasts as you like. The vast majority of them are free, but there are a handful for which you have to pay a subscription.

Podcasts can be on any topic and include just about any content, other than copyrighted material to which you don't have the rights. They can also be any length and as frequent or infrequent as you wish. Most are between 15 minutes and an hour and come out weekly or monthly. People listen to them on iPods or other MP3 players or on their computers. They can also burn them to CDs and listen to them on their car sound systems.

If you have an Apple Mac computer, you can easily create podcasts using GarageBand, one component of the inexpensive iLife software set. It is configured for podcasts and allows you to easily record your voice, add jingles and introductory music (included with the program and copyright free), and edit the material you have recorded.

Some people hesitate to start a podcast because they don't have a trained radio voice. It's not essential that you sound like a polished radio performer; what really matters is whether people want to listen to the content and, as with a blog, whether the podcaster's personality comes through. If those two elements are in place, listeners will overlook a less-than-stellar voice and imperfect production. In fact, I think it works in your favor if you don't sound like all those smooth-tongued radio announcers.

To keep people interested, break up the podcast into small segments, just as you'd break up big chunks of text. For audio, you can use a sound effect or a brief bit of music to create some variety. You can also feature interviews with other people, or have a friend or colleague read short items. Some podcasts feature a quiz or other interactive feature, with people sending their answers in via email to win a prize or just be mentioned on the next podcast. This can be an effective way to get people coming back for the following episode.

Other than creative expression, what's the point of doing a podcast? Some have ads on their associated websites, but again this is not a serious source of income for more than a few people. The benefits of podcasting are very similar to those of a blog: You reach a lot of people, you gain credibility in your arena, and you can get feedback from your listeners. Because the production process is more involved, there are fewer podcasts than blogs, so you have less competition, but there are also fewer users. At this writing, I'm in the process of getting together the Your Writing Coach podcast, which will be live by the time you read this book, so please check it out.

You can also create video blogs (sometimes called vlogs), which are video versions of a podcast. Again, the iLife software is useful because it includes a video editing program called iMovies, which is easy to use, yet quite sophisticated for its price. You can also create short films and upload them free to sites like Google and YouTube. I've uploaded several animations to these, with an end title card that contains my website address. Because there are hundreds of thousands of new videos uploaded every week, it's easy for yours to get lost at sites like this. On the other hand, the audience is so huge that if your video catches on, you could reach an enormous number of people. Also, you can put a link to your Google or YouTube video on your website or blog, so that people are taken directly to it. This way, you don't need to store the video on the server you're using, nor pay for the bandwidth used when lots of people access your video.

Feeding the hungry animals

The only real drawback to blogs and podcasts is that they devour material. To have a meaningful presence you will have to be consistent in adding new posts regularly. What is fun for the first few weeks can turn into a demanding routine after a while. There may be days or weeks when you just can't think of much you want to say, but if you don't add content, your audience may switch to sites that do. On most blogging hosts you can write an entry and then schedule it to go live at a future date, and I recommend that you always work a couple of entries ahead. That way if you do need to pause for a week or so, the flow will still continue.

Another option is to share a blog or podcast with one or more people who have similar interests, and set up a rota so each of you adds something new once a week, for example. If you do this, each person posting should identify who has written that particular post, so as not to confuse your readers. You don't need to agree on everything; in fact, a bit of conflict can make a blog or podcast more interesting, just as it makes those movie reviews more interesting when one of the reviewers gives it a thumbs up and the other gives it a thumbs down.

Your new media strategy

It should be clear from this chapter that the new media are real, and they're coming your way. You have to decide whether to embrace them and ride the wave, or to let others be the pioneers. As your writing coach, I strongly advise you to do the former.

What does this mean in practical terms?

First, resolve to educate yourself further about new media by reading newspapers (most now have a weekly technology section) and magazines (including *Wired*, *Fast Company*, and *Forbes*) for articles about the newest approaches and their impact on the media scene. Regularly check news, media, and technology websites.

Second, master the basic skills required for creating blogs, podcasts, and websites (but outsource the technical side of things if they don't interest you or represent the best use of your time).

Then establish an internet presence for yourself in as many ways as make sense for the kind of writing you are doing. A simple website is the minimum price of entry, a blog is an easily added component, and an audio or video podcast might be a good idea. Remember that all of these are effective only if they are seen, and use the guerrilla marketing techniques in this book to drive eyes and ears to your sites.

Third, be an active consumer of the media for which you might want to write. Buy some e-books, get a games machine (or find a child who is willing to show you how to use his or hers), check out the new made-for-the-web programs. From this point on, surfing the web becomes research (you may show this sentence to your spouse or significant other).

Fourth, when you are creating a new project, consider from the start which medium would be best for it. If it's a book, for example, does it fit in with what traditional publishers are looking for? Or does it have niche appeal that makes it a good candidate for self-publishing? If the latter, what fits best: printing hard copies, using print on demand, or turning it into an e-book? Also consider at the start how many ways you might be able to re-purpose material. For example, when I was doing interviews for this book, I realized that it would be useful to put audio clips from them on my podcast, so I recorded them with a high-quality digital recorder. With the interviews I did on video, I now have the option of putting the videos on my website, the audio tracks on my podcast, and transcribed excerpts on my blog. Another example: Years ago I started a scriptwriting newsletter called *The Hollywood Scriptwriter* (which still exists, but under different ownership). In each issue I featured an in-depth interview. Later I was able to reuse much of that material for a book called *Top Secrets: Screenwriting*, co-written with Kerry Cox.

Finally, any time you see a new outlet that might have use for the kind of writing you do, be proactive and make contact. As was mentioned earlier, with the new media the barriers to entry are much lower and the methods for getting in are not yet well established. Like the young songwriter who sold his lyrics line by line, or the Japanese short story writer, you have to be imaginative and enterprising, and you may be surprised at what you can achieve.

KEY POINTS

- New forms of film, television, newspaper, and magazine content are springing up, offering fresh opportunities for writers.
- Book authors have a range of different ways to get their work out, including self-publishing, print on demand, and e-books. The latter two require a very low investment and therefore carry little risk.
- The rules for how to get into new media have not yet been formed, therefore you have to be imaginative, enterprising, and proactive.
- You should have an internet presence, at the very least a website, preferably also a blog, possibly also an audio or video podcast.
- To take advantage of the new media, you need to interact with them.

EXERCISES

- Go into a large electronics store and check out the latest devices. If you feel intimidated but want to benefit from the new markets, find a teenager to clue you in.
- Brainstorm whether the four case studies in this chapter hold any lessons that could be applied to you and what you write.
- If you don't yet have a website, surf the web looking at other writers' sites, note which features you find attractive and effective, and figure out how to adopt or adapt them to your own site.

✐ Sign up for free newsletters at the tech and new media-oriented websites.

CHAPTER BONUS

On the website www.yourwritingcoach.com, click on the "Chapter Bonuses" tab, then the "New Media" tab, and type in the code: media. You will be taken a page that contains a round-up of current news regarding opportunities for writers targeting new media.

18

The Writing Life

"There are two things to aim at in life: first, to get what you want; and, after that, to enjoy it. Only the wisest of mankind achieve the second."

—*Logan Piersall Smith*

If you've worked your way through the previous chapters with me, you now have figured out what you want to write, how to write it, and how to market it. In this final chapter, I want to share with you some strategies for establishing and sustaining a successful writing career.

Keep setting and reaching goals

Motivation guru Brian Tracey tells the story of his life-changing experience: He was traveling across the Sahara with friends when their Land Rover broke down. They were low on water and they knew that if they couldn't fix the car they'd die. Tracey says:

> *"That's when something locked in. I realized I was responsible for my own life. I stopped blaming my parents, my teachers, other people. I knew nothing in my life would ever change unless I changed; I knew a person in this life must be a proactive agent in his life rather than a reactive agent."*

Here is Tracey's prescription for being effectively proactive:

"You must be clear about the goals you set, flexible about the process of achieving them, and then continually learn all you can in every way possible."

The best way to stay on track is to review your goals monthly. If what you're doing to move toward that goal isn't working, decide what you can do differently, and identify what would be helpful for you to learn in the coming month.

Stay flexible

Although I believe strongly in setting goals, it's also important to keep your eyes open for unexpected opportunities. Sometimes people get so fixated on a specific goal that they don't even notice that something else, which might give them just as much, if not more, money and satisfaction, is available for the taking.

Traditional approaches to setting and reaching goals say you should focus so much on your goal that you filter out all other possibilities, but in a chaotic and unpredictable climate this may be exactly the wrong strategy. One way to maintain flexibility is to make sure that when you review your progress toward the goal, you also ask yourself whether it is still important to you. Otherwise you may find, as one executive said, "I spent years climbing the ladder and finally got to the top... only to find it was leaning against the wrong wall." Also, when a new opportunity comes up that clashes with your goal, carefully examine whether it might be worth pursuing even if it means delaying or discarding your current goal.

Expect obstacles

Some writers assume that once they have had their first breakthrough, for example having a novel published, their troubles are at an end. I have a favorite Zen story about people and problems:

A farmer went to see the Buddha about his various problems: The weather was either too hot and it dried out his crops, or too wet and it caused floods, and his wife didn't understand him, and his son was ungrateful and rebellious. The Buddha said he couldn't help because all human beings have 83 problems. A few may go away, but soon enough others take their place. So we will always have 83 problems.

The farmer was indignant. "Then what is the good of all your teaching?" he demanded.

The Buddha said, "My teaching can't help with the 83 problems, but perhaps it can help with the 84th."

"What's that?" the farmer asked.

"The 84th problem," the Buddha said, "is that we don't want to have any problems."

The reality is that every writing career, just like every other career, has ups and downs. You can have a great success and then something happens that throws you off. Maybe an editor or producer who loves your work gets fired, retires, or dies, or the production company that wanted to make your movie goes bankrupt, or a magazine folds without paying you for work you've already done (I've experienced all of these). Of course, you must take sensible precautions, but some things will always be out of your control, and if you accept that you will find the setbacks easier to take.

Be your own role model

When you do encounter an obstacle that leaves you at a loss about how to proceed, consider being your own role model. One of the hot areas in management and self-development is "modeling"; that is, observing how experts do what they do, and then doing the same things. However, it's even easier to model yourself. Here's how.

Make two columns on a piece of paper. In one column, write down all the things you do really well (not just in your work, but in any area of your life). In the second column, list the problem or obstacle you're facing. Now look at how you approach the things you do well and consider how that might translate to dealing with the situations in the second column. For example, if you are really good at keeping your office tidy but not at writing query letters, what can you apply from the first experience to the second? Combine different pairs until you find a model that might work, then try it out.

Sometimes winners do quit

Have you heard the saying, "Winners never quit, and quitters never win?" In general, perseverance and determination are great qualities for a writer. However, sometimes knowing when to quit is also a powerful asset.

I had a painful reminder of this not so long ago. I wrote a television series for Germany that the director, with the backing of the producer, changed a lot, for the worse. In my heart I knew I should quit the project and take my name off it, but I rationalized my way out of that decision. The outcome: The series flopped... with my name still on it. The moral: Trust your vision and be true to yourself. When it's no longer possible to do that within a particular situation, get out.

Here's what director Tim Burton had to say about this in a recent interview:

> "There was a very specific moment in my life when I had a breakthrough. I was at the California Institute of Arts, and I had been getting more and more exasperated because I was trying to fit into a certain style of drawing—the Disney way—and I almost had a breakdown, and I was just sitting there and I said, 'You know what? I can't draw like this. I'm just gonna draw whatever way I draw and that's it.' And at

that moment, my drawings changed. In one second, I drew completely different. In a different style and a different way. It was like a drug experience—literally, my mind expanded."

Turn troubles into assets

An article in *The Times* (London) told how a writer named Clare Allan used her writing to deal with her mental illness. She said, "Writing helped me recover. You need a purpose in life and for me that was crucial." Writing also changed her attitude toward the distressing times she had: "You can be having the worst experience in your life and a bit of you is thinking, 'Ooh, that'll be a good story.'"

Allen's first book, *Poppy Shakespeare*, is based partly on her experiences, but writing that never gets published can still be a great outlet. There's something about putting down your experiences, whether as a journal or transformed into fiction, that allows you to take a healthy step back from them.

Stay true to yourself

In other chapters I've already warned against trying to write to suit current fads rather than your own vision. Naturally, you have to pay attention to the marketplace, but the real breakthroughs often are the projects that offer something new and different. Here's a surprising story of what happened when one person decided to go her own way.

Young artist Erin Crowe found the face of former Federal Reserve Board Chairman Alan Greenspan interesting, and for two years she painted a variety of portraits of him, based on photos. When she needed to raise some money before going off to graduate school, she decided to try selling some of them. Family friends owned a gallery in New York, and agreed to host a show of her Greenspan paintings. According to *The Artist's Magazine*:

"no one was prepared for what happened next. CNBC did a piece on Crowe's gallery show, and it went from moderately successful to sold-out in a few short hours. Bankers, hedge fund managers and other Wall Street types lined up to buy her oil paintings of the famous financial figure."

If you truly believe in what you are doing, sometimes it pays to go with your impulse, even it's totally new or just plain weird.

Be bold

A related point to being true to your vision is being bold. Recently I attended a life drawing class, where one of the main points made by the instructor is that we should draw big. Even with a large piece of paper in front of us, many of us started to draw a little figure, maybe because we're used to writing or drawing on smaller sheets of paper. At first daunting, using the entire page is quite exhilarating after a while.

There's something in that for us as writers, too: Do we habitually "write small"? How often do we step back and see the larger canvas and decide to go for making the bigger, bolder mark? This could mean taking on a bigger theme than you normally dare to, or writing more colorfully, or creating a character that fully reflects your shadow side.

Remember what's really important

As much as I hope that you will make a lot of money from your writing, it's possible that you will encounter some lean years. There may be times when you wonder whether you should go back to the day job that you didn't enjoy but that brought in more money. Here's a thought-provoking passage written by someone who goes by the name of Psy, in an issue of *Reclaiming Quarterly* magazine:

"Imagine that a rich relative left you an inheritance. There is enough money that you never have to work again if you keep your expenses low by sharing an apartment with roommates, using the bus instead of owning a car, cooking your meals at home, and so on. What would you do with your time? Would you work at all? Learn to play the piano?... Be a full-time parent? Where do your passions lie? Why aren't you following those passions right now? Why aren't you living that life? Is your path in life more important than living a lifestyle that obscures it? Can you make some changes to your lifestyle to rebuild your life around your passions? Will you?"

If writing is really important to you, it could be worth making some sacrifices in order to allow yourself to keep going with it.

As well as deciding how to spend money, it's vital to be aware how you're spending your time. I've already addressed this in another chapter, but it's so important that I want to reiterate it, because it's easy to lose sight of it when we encounter other time pressures.

Here's what top executive Nandan Kilekani (CEO of Infosys) told *Fortune* magazine about his attitude to time: "I have a saying—I am generous with my money and stingy with my time. I think time is the most important asset I have."

All too often, we count our pennies but waste our minutes (or hours). If you begin to fall behind in your writing, ask yourself what you could stop doing, or pay someone else to do, in order to have more time to write.

This isn't goodbye

We've come to the end of this book, but not the end of our connection. I've set out to be your writing coach, and I hope as time goes on you will refer to this book again, to help you through any rough spots or inspire you when you start a new project. If you haven't done so, be sure to make use of all the chapter bonuses on the website www.yourwritingcoach.com. There you will also be able to contact me via email. If you have a problem I can help with, let me know, and please also tell me about your writing successes. I look forward to hearing from you.

KEY POINTS

- Setting and pursuing goals must be balanced with the flexibility required to take advantage of unexpected opportunities.
- Obstacles are a normal part of the writing life, but one way we can overcome them is to use our past successes in any aspects of our lives as a model.
- Sometimes quitting is a good idea.
- Be bold.

EXERCISES

- Goals tend to evaporate unless they are written down, have a target date, and are measurable. Make a chart showing your three top goals, when you expect to reach them, and how you'll measure your progress toward them.
- When you read a newspaper or magazine, put on the filter of "What opportunity will I find in this material today?" Keep a log of your ideas and act on the best ones.

CHAPTER BONUS

On the website www.yourwritingcoach.com, click on the "Chapter Bonuses" tab, then the "Life" tab, and type in the code: life. You will be taken to a video interview with... me. I'll be talking about crafting your long-term career as a writer.